# Know Your Audience

# 10X Your Speaking Business

# Know Your Audience

## 10X Your Speaking Business

Douglas Vermeeren

**YouSpeakIt**

P U B L I S H I N G

*The Easy Way
to Get Your Book
Done Right*™

www.YouSpeakItPublishing.com

*This book is dedicated to Markus and Dezz.*
*You guys are my biggest reasons why.*

# *Acknowledgments*

I would especially like to acknowledge all the speakers who have come before to make today's personal development business possible. So many stellar speakers have made this a viable career for many of us, it is nearly impossible to list them all. I'd like to personally acknowledge a few who have made a difference to me:

Brian Tracy, the first speaker I introduced at a professional event;

John Demartini, a close friend, mentor, and inspiration;

Bob Proctor, an industry leader who has forged the path and touched so many of us;

Jack Canfield, Mark Victor Hansen, Joe Vitale, Bob Doyle, Marci Shimoff, Bill Bartmann, Bill Farley, Morris Goodman, Frank Maguire, and all the rest of our crew at *The Opus*;

John Gray, Mary Morrissey, Joe Rubino, and our gang at *The Gratitude Experiment*;

And, of course, Raymond Aaron, Loral Langmeier, Marshall Sylver, Randy Gage, Stefan Arnio, Darren Jacklin, and our gang from *The Treasure Map*.

There are many other powerful speakers who have influenced me and inspired me to become a better speaker. I know I've left out a ton of people. But I do want to say I love you all. Thank you.

Thanks to Maura and Keith Leon at YouSpeakIt Publishing for creating the process that made it so easy to get this book done.

And then there's my wife, Holly. She gets her own paragraph—without her I could do nothing. I always let my audiences know that most of my best material comes from our conversations together. I don't know of a smarter woman on the planet. Holly, you are amazing and I love you.

# *Foreword*

The timing of this book is perfect.

If ever there were a time when it was important to get clear about your divine purpose, and to step fully into it, it's now. We come this way but once. We can either tiptoe through life and hope that we get to death without being too badly bruised, or we can live a full, complete life, achieving our goals and realizing our wildest dreams. The author of this book is a living demonstration that you can do, be, or have anything you want in this life.

It's amazing what Douglas Vermeeren has accomplished. He's directed and appeared in three inspiring personal development films and authored books and series, such as *Guerilla Marketing* and *For Dummies*. More importantly, regarding the subject of this book, he's used the movies and books as a platform to build a motivational speaking platform. He shares his mission and message with rooms filled with people who are perfectly ready to hear the message.

It's important to me that anyone I endorse understands the concept of a *paradigm shift*. When I changed my paradigm back in 1961, my life changed like night and day.

To change a paradigm, it's important to do two things:

1.  You've got to learn how to make decisions.

2.  You've got to learn how to make money.

The more money you have, the more effective you can become. The more effective you become, the more people you'll be able to support in their own growth. This book not only teaches how to build a speaking business, but it also dives deeply into the *why's* and *how's*. You'll become clear on what your unique message is, why it's important for you to share it, and how to get on stages to share your story.

In this book, Doug teaches you to select the speaking opportunities that best support your mission and your message. He discusses speaking fee options, speaking venue possibilities, event hosting considerations, and marketing. Doug shares his personal experiences with you in a very straightforward and understandable way.

Truly, there are no mistakes. If you're holding this book in your hands right now, you were born to be a difference maker. Now is the time to step into the greatness of all you are here to be. Speaking your truth and sharing your stories are great ways to make a difference in this world. Keep taking bold steps forward, follow the steps laid out in this book, and you'll be able to share your mission and message with those who are ready to hear it, at the most perfect time.

The good things in life are not always easy. When you really want something, and you couple that with an understanding of your nature, your spiritual being, and the laws that govern you, you will keep going, regardless of what has happened. Nothing will stop you.

Every one of us is hardwired to do something phenomenal with our life. Every last one of us is destined for greatness. The only thing that gets in our way is our own negative thoughts and programming. To change your life, you've got to change the channel. Start reading and listening to things that will support a positive change, and the world will change around you. You must change a paradigm in the same way it was created — through repetition of information. This book encourages paradigm-shifting behavior. I suggest you read this book over and over again.

To your success,

Bob Proctor

Author, Speaker, and Featured Teacher in the hit movie, *The Secret*

# Contents

# *Introduction*

The speaking, coaching, and training business is one of the fastest-growing industries in the world today.

Many people would like to break into this business for various reasons. They've been inspired by a speaker they had a chance to see, or maybe they've had experiences in their own lives that could benefit others. They may even have business solutions that others need.

I've been a professional speaker for quite some time, and I've met a lot of people who have incredible tools to share. But, not all of them get a chance to create successful speaking businesses, for one reason or another. Most of the time, it's because they do not have the tools to build the business. They have the *content,* what they want to offer, but they don't have the *skills and knowledge* required to build the elements of a business.

This book walks you through the steps of how to evaluate potential speaking events.

You will learn to:

- Evaluate the audiences you want to share with
- Discover the problems you actually can solve
- Determine how to make a profit and navigate this world of speaking

That's the essence of this book.

The information comes from my own personal experiences, which include:

- Building a multi-million-dollar speaking business over the last decade

- Sharing the stage with multiple A-list speakers

- Creating media opportunities for myself as a speaker

- Appearing in three of the top personal development films of all time

- Authoring books and series, such as *Guerilla Marketing* and *For Dummies*

The advice and experiences I share are ideas and strategies that you can count on to work for you in your daily life. If you are not receiving the recognition that you deserve, your brilliance may be getting lost. Your lessons need to be shared, but perhaps you haven't been able to take your business to the next level. My goal is to help you and your business deliver those brilliant messages and excellent solutions so they can elevate everyone.

You might be holding yourself back. Even though you've got great information, maybe you're not sure if you should enter into this business. Maybe it's too complex, competitive, or lacking in opportunity for you. If you follow the principles outlined in this book, you will find a spot in this business.

Mastery equals monopoly, so don't worry about the competition. Get good at your own thing; get good at serving your audience. As you master it, you'll find that your audience will find you and competition will not matter.

To achieve the best results, have a notepad alongside you as you read, and start writing down strategies that come to mind for your own business.

As I share a particular principle, ask yourself how would you put it into practice in your own business.

How can you use this information as a group, such as in a *mastermind* or *joint-venturing setting* — which we'll talk more about later — to build better events and opportunities for yourself as a speaker?

Lastly, it's important to revisit this book often. As your speaking business changes, grows, and evolves, so will your answers and insights into the questions and strategies I present. You'll notice in some sections I talk about what high-level speakers are doing, and maybe you're not there yet. Maybe you'll be there in a year, or two, or more. I've designed the book so that certain elements will be more relevant and accessible to you as your business grows.

At the age of nineteen, as a new speaker, I earned $1.6 million in business! People often approach me and ask if they can sit with me and learn how I created a multi-million-dollar speaking business.

They want to know how I've managed to accomplish so much, such as:

- Appearing frequently on media as a thought leader

- Becoming the go-to guy for media outlets like Fox, Fox Business, CNN, and NBC

- Being featured on magazine covers and in various magazine articles

- Signing book deals

- Forging joint ventures with some of the top speakers in the world

- Producing movies

Due to time and financial constrictions, I'm not able to take the time to mentor everyone one-on-one.

The carefully selected strategies shared in this book are the vital ones to help you achieve the best results in the shortest time possible. You will have the tools that you need to become profitable, visible, and relevant in today's speaking market.

My one-on-one students pay upwards of $100,000 a year to go through this information with me. They see results. Their businesses grow based on the results that we help them obtain. If you apply these ideas to your situation, you will have a more profitable and successful speaking business. If you do these things correctly, you'll also find that you'll have a more balanced business. This allows you to focus on the art of speaking, more so than putting out fires, chasing paychecks, and sprinting after speaking gigs like most people do. You will be able to run a sustainable business with predictable outcomes.

# CHAPTER ONE

---

# Selecting Opportunities

## MATCH YOUR MESSAGE TO YOUR AUDIENCE

Speakers generally try to position themselves as the *thought leaders* — those individuals others trust for advice, expertise, and direction. A common challenge is that they are trying to be too many things to too many people. There's the old saying that when you try to become a jack-of-all-trades, you essentially become a master of none. If you're trying to find the right audience for your message, you must clarify what your message and expertise are. It's not simply a matter of teaching a subject; you need to have the skills and knowledge behind it.

For example, if you were a high school janitor, you might not be best suited to teach leadership principles to high-level CEOs. As much as you love that topic, you don't necessarily have the experience, the knowledge, the skills, or the ability to teach at that level.

We assume, sometimes incorrectly, that any audience can support our business. We assume that, as long as we stand in front of people as a speaker, we will be successful. Finding the right audience for your message gives you the ability to understand more deeply how to serve that group, how to market to that group, and the problems that this group encounters. The more equipped you are to be specific and focused, the more you can zero in on finding that ideal group. Then everything becomes easier—whether it's marketing, product creation, presentations, or monetization. Everything becomes easier once you have a clear view of the ideal audience.

Think of your business as a funnel; most people picture the funnel with the wide end at the top and the narrow end at the bottom. In this picture, they're doing more at the top, seeking more speaking opportunities, but ultimately, they're getting less. The better way in this business is to put the funnel upside down, with the narrow end on top, becoming extremely focused on the correct audience. Building boundaries around what *isn't* correct allows you to focus on what *is* the right audience. Ultimately, you gain more. If you think of the inverted funnel, it expands and fans out more when we become more focused at the beginning, the top.

## Identify the Problems

Consider these questions:

- Why do people engage with speakers?
- Why do they hire thought leaders?
- Why do they hire a coach to help them get to the next level in life or in business?

Well, it's because they have problems they need to solve. The more relevant and painful the problem, the more people are willing to pay to have that problem solved.

If it's an irrelevant problem, there's no purpose in finding a solution, right?

I've often used the analogy that if someone held a seminar about, for example, how to color-coordinate your Beanie Babies collection, or categorize your bottle caps, no one would care. Those are not relevant problems that affect our lives in a significant way. An audience for that seminar is not going to pay a lot and will be small in comparison to a seminar on a problem that's quite significant in people's lives—issues and topics that they can connect directly to a tangible result, whether it's in their day-to-day lives, careers, finances, or relationships. If the problem is significant, and the results that they can anticipate will be significant, people will dial in a solution.

The reason people purchase anything — when it comes to speaking or training — is based on what they say to themselves, and how they see their futures.

These two things affect purchase decisions:

1. What people say to themselves
2. How they see their futures

If people have a problem that won't make a big difference in their futures, then they already say to themselves: *Well, I've got that solved.* They're not prepared to take any kind of action or do anything differently.

However, if they have a problem and say to themselves:

- *I can't handle this on my own.*
- *I need support.*
- *The information that the speaker is sharing makes sense to me as a viable solution.*

Then, they picture themselves in the future, implementing that solution and achieving a better result, and they will do business with you. It revolves around people's ability to solve specific problems.

Often, inexperienced speakers, or speakers who aren't being compensated as much as they'd like, focus on problems that everyone else is addressing, as well as on surface-area problems. I assign my students to make a of list twenty-five problems that they solve for their clients, rather than just a few. Most people can come up with ten pretty easily. That's basic: they are the surface problems. Once you reach number fifteen, you need to think a lot deeper and explore problems that most people don't think about. Then, as you're reaching twenty or twenty-five, you're becoming an expert on what your clients encounter.

We don't spend enough time thinking about the very real problems that cost our clients time, money, opportunity, and maybe even reputation. Therefore, because we haven't considered those problems, we've not found solutions. The expert who has taken the time to consider these deeper problems will have a higher caliber of solution, and therefore, they're going to find this whole process of becoming positioned as an expert or a thought leader or running standing-room-only seminars much easier. It will happen automatically once your level of expertise deepens, to the point where your audience truly understands that you are the person with the solutions they're looking for.

**Demographics: Understand Your Audience**

You've probably heard of the *Pareto Principle,* or the *80/20 Rule.* It is true in this business, as well, that in your audience, 20 percent will be your absolute best clients.

Most speakers haven't worked to understand these people: everything from their age, gender, occupation, and financial background to the problems that they're trying to solve. And even if you can access or collect this information, you may not have made the effort to market specifically to them and increase your base of ideal clients.

Don't be satisfied with simply identifying the 20 percent, but actually *fire* the other 80 percent. Work with the 20 percent, your ideal clients, and in that group of 20 percent, you'll also find another 80/20 split. Over time, get rid of *that* 80 percent, and always fine-tune your audience.

I'll speak to big groups, but most of my funding, resources, products, and so forth are always directed to the 20 percent of the 20 percent, and so on. This is so I can find the absolutely best people to work with. I recently held an event in London, where seven people attended.

Most people would say: *That's not really a big speaking event. How can you make a lot of money with only seven people in a room?*

Well, if they are the right people—the 20 percent of the 20 percent, of the 20 percent, of the 20 percent— you can do quite well. In that room, I made £260,000. The exchange rate at the time was equivalent to nearly

$500,000. When you understand the clients you are serving, it exponentially amplifies your ability to be of service.

Does that make sense?

To find your ideal clients, you need to do more than understand your client demographics. Although you may spend time identifying the physical attributes of the numbers, or the specifics and the details of who they are, you need to spend more time thinking about how your clients feel when they come to you. You also need to decide how you're going to relate with them, and how you're going to approach them so that they feel good.

Coaches and speakers often say to me, "I know who my client is. I know their age, their sex, the whole bit."

I don't think they know how their clients feel when they're arriving at an event:

- Where have they just come from?
- What are they experiencing in their day-to-day lives?
- What emotions are they are experiencing?

When I conduct a seminar, one of the things I do as people arrive is imagine the worst-case scenario. Maybe a woman walking in had a big fight with her husband. Maybe on the way, she got a flat tire.

How is she distracted?

Then I use that — what are they most likely feeling when they arrive — to lead them into a more unified feeling. I find that a simple instruction causes a *state change* — a shift in the energy level of the room — bringing them into a sense of feeling seen and understood, knowing that I'm there as a support.

The long and short of it is we're not only looking for the specifics of the statistics. We're looking, also, to understand these people as real and genuine.

## Clear and Recognizable Message

If you don't understand your own message, your audience certainly won't. You need clarity about what problem you solve, whom you're serving, and how you're going to serve them. The more clarity you achieve, the better. I systematize my own content, so that at any time I'm meeting with a student, I can see where they are on the continuum. If they express certain challenges or concerns, I can also see how to move them from where they are to where they want to be.

Gaining clarity about your message also involves understanding the problems that you solve and the solutions that work. If you can address these questions clearly, and they express certain challenges or concerns, your audience will have more confidence in you. They'll know that you've experienced the journey, and they'll trust you enough to follow you there.

Another aspect of clarity is developing purpose, not just with your message, but individually, as a presenter and as a teacher. People follow those who communicate they have a purpose. When you embody your purpose, potential clients see that, and they're willing to trust you for the solutions to the challenges they face.

You need to be clear about why you're teaching what you're teaching, why you've chosen this idea as a speaker, a coach, or a trainer. In other words, why you're here and what you're sharing.

You'll also need to build recognition among your audience. There are a lot of voices in the marketplace, sharing a lot of ideas. One of the biggest challenges and concerns I face is with people who call themselves a *life coach,* a *business coach,* or a *goal-setting coach.*

What do those terms mean?

There are so many different aspects of life, business, or even goal setting. When someone tells me that's what they do, I know they haven't gone deep enough to find clarity about what problems they're solving for clients.

Even if you take one aspect of life—let's say relationships—how deep could you go within the topic of relationships to gain clarification?

Some people teach about how to improve marriage relationships. So, now they're even more specific: life, relationships, and now marriage.

What about marriage?

Well, you can go deeper.

What if somebody's been in an abusive situation?

It's like peeling the layers of an onion. The deeper you get toward the center, the more clarity you'll have.

Too many people try to stay comfortable at the generic level:

- I serve everyone, and I can help everyone.
- *I've taken a coaching program,* or *I speak a little bit.*
- *I can show you how to set goals, manage your time, or improve your life.*

They haven't dug into the depths of developing their business, so their audience cannot recognize them when they appear on the scene.

When we talk about egoist titles in a later chapter, you will begin to define your audience. As your message and purpose become clearer to you *and* your audience, you will find each other. That's recognition.

It's not enough to be a speaker and teacher. Your goal isn't to speak to *everyone* and draw the biggest audience in the world. If you're going to be profitable, successful, and position yourself as an expert, your goal is to attract and find those who resonate with you and your message. Achieving clarity allows those people to recognize that they are a good fit with you. The sooner you can do it, the more successful you'll be!

## MATCH AUDIENCE TO NEEDS

Many people begin their speaking or coaching business without planning the monetization end. They start coaching because — and I hate to say it — they've been inspired by watching a personal development movie, or reading a book, or maybe even attending an event or a coaching session themselves. Right away, they are inspired, and they go out and start speaking and teaching.

They start without planning how to run a business or a career for themselves. The challenge is making a profit; without a profit, you don't earn the privilege to continue. As with anything in life, money is the admission ticket to be able to move forward. If you aren't providing value in such a way that you can be compensated for it, you won't get the opportunity to stick around for very long.

Many speakers I know believe that if they're going to be a healer or a helper, they must turn their back on money — it can't be something they focus on.

Wallace D. Wattles, in *The Science of Getting Rich*, says:

> Whatever may be said in praise of poverty, the fact remains that a person is not truly successful until they are rich. If you are trying to share with someone how to build a more abundant, prosperous, insightful, and rewarding life, part of that is going to be financial compensation, because money is really a more tangible way to measure those kinds of energies in life.

Remember the old saying: *If somebody tells you that money's not really that important or money isn't everything, you can guarantee that they're broke.*

People who provide high value, maintain high energy levels, and develop high-abundance thinking are going to naturally be very wealthy, as well. This is what you're leading other people to do. If you want your clients to be healthy, wealthy, well, and fit, or to have all the abundance possible in their lives, you're going to have to accept those things for yourself first. You must create it for yourself first, before you can create it for others.

It's like another old saying: *A lifeguard can't help anyone else until they know how to swim.*

If you're teaching people to be the best they can be, finances are one area that can't be neglected, right?

You need to have your own success there, as well.

## Offer Messages in Digestible Pieces

There are three ways to approach this:

1. **Package your message effectively.** It needs to be packaged in pieces that can be easily defined and absorbed. It can't be an abstract: *Okay, we're going to get together and discuss these principles, and maybe it will cost this much, or maybe it will cost this much.*

    It's helpful to think of it as a menu, where your message is available in sizeable chunks, and clients can begin the journey and relationship with you. One of the key points about monetization of your business is that it's about relationships first. Your customers must have an emotional connection with you.

You might be thinking: *Well, what do you mean? That's more important than the content?*

Yes, the relationship is the most important piece, because people will not connect or learn from someone they do not like and trust. So, that emotional connection is number one.

2. **The content must make sense and be valuable.** It must solve the problem that you've identified.

3. **Your clients need to see results.** I know that sounds weird. Some people will insist that results come first. If the content doesn't make sense, people won't try it, so they'll never get to the results. And if they didn't like you, they won't listen to content.

These three things are necessary for a successful client relationship:

- The emotional connection
- The content
- The results

In my coaching and speaking business, I use a target as a visual of my business. The closer clients get to the center — meaning me — the more time they spend with me and the more direct influence they receive from me. I recognize that these services need to be priced accordingly. To schedule one-on-one time with me, especially with my personal life and my family life, comes at a price. I am not open and available twenty-four hours a day, seven days a week. I couldn't possibly serve a large number of people.

So, at the outer ring of my imaginary target are products and services I offer that don't require my presence: books, audio programs, videos, and online courses. They're priced accessibly for people because I don't have to be there to service the products. However, as clients move toward the center of the ring—let's say they attend an event and get a little time with me—the price is going to increase.

As they approach the bull's-eye, perhaps they will enroll in one of my one-on-one mentoring programs, in which I actually work with speakers. In my program for the Speaking Business Multiplier or High Profit Speaker, clients spend an hour a week with me, one-on-one. I only take ten of those students. Well, as you can imagine, the cost to be part of that program can sometimes be as high as $100,000.

These types of programs and services can be planned, digestible, and easily packaged, but you should also take into consideration your time, availability, and desires. For instance, with some of my more intensive programs, I've made a conscious decision about certain types of speakers I want to work with, and about other industries or speaking topics that I'm not as excited about. I can set up those boundaries as well, so that I'm bringing in clients or discussion topics that I'm interested in.

We want to create programs for clients that they can consume and experience—the emotional connection, the content, and the results. It must be digestible in that way. You can build your menu of programs and services in such a way that it's systematized as much as possible. If you know where you're going with each of the elements and pieces, you can see its natural development along the way. Moving forward, you can help people understand where they're going and, if they have specific problems, you can even point out which elements of the program can help them.

## Affordable Offerings

Let's look again at the target. The closer to the bull's-eye on the target, the larger the monetary investment from clients. When people make a financial decision, they're contemplating several things. First, they want to try you out and build the relationship. I'm a firm believer that you need to offer something that's accessible for clients to try you out. Naturally, as they experience the results and they're finding value, they're more likely to spend more.

A statistic I've heard is that when people buy from you the first time, they're probably 10 percent more likely to buy from you a second time. But, after buying from you a second time, this increases to about 55 percent. Those who buy from you a third time are 75 percent likely to say yes to anything you offer. And those who buy from you a fourth time will, generally, buy anything you're bringing through the door, as long as the dates and the finances work.

At some of these sell-a-thon events, speakers sell programs from the stage that are $2,000, $3,000, even $5,000 or $10,000. This strategy may work for some, but these speakers often experience a high rate of refund requests, because people feel like they bought it in the excitement of the moment rather than seeing the value in it. Or later they're disappointed, feeling they didn't get the $5,000 or $10,000 value.

I prefer to focus on the relationship. I start my pricing quite small to make sure that I create an irresistible offer, where clients receive extreme value, so they will continue over time. Rather than looking at a customer as a purchasing event — *I can get $2,000 out of this person* — I look at them as a relationship and consider it a lifetime investment. If they continue with me over the course of five, ten, or more years, the compensation will be quite dramatic. My income will be quite different than the $2,000 that a coach sold at the sell-a-thon event. It doesn't take long to get into the $2,000 range once people have experienced and found value.

Speakers who are comfortable offering long-term relationships are confident of the value they provide over the long term. *Pump and Dump* events get everybody excited and sell a program but are never heard from again. The reason is they don't have anything further to offer beyond that first event.

I want to make sure that the audience can afford to buy the experience that's valuable to them. To create my pricing, I look at the potential return for these people, and I like to have a return that's roughly three times the cost of the event. For example, if I calculate that my program will help a client do $30,000 in business, then I'm justified charging $10,000 for it. But if I can't see that they could quickly and quite easily turn what they learn into $30,000, then I'm going to reduce the price.

Many of my introductory events start at $197, and I offer some that start at $1,000. But I generally don't offer anything as a first-time program with me that would be much pricier than that because I believe clients need time to build the relationship with me. I know that some people sell programs for more, and they do perfectly well. Other people's offerings are inexpensive, but they're not providing value to clients. The key is not the dollar amount, per se. The key is that your audience needs to receive return on their investment. Your audience thinks in terms of an investment and not an expense.

They shouldn't be looking at your events as: *How much does this cost?*

They should be looking at it from the perspective of: *What am I going to gain from it, and does that make sense based on the cost?*

If it makes sense, then the actual dollar figure— whatever you're charging—is irrelevant.

I offer some high-cost, one-on-one coaching experiences, and making this affordable for my clients can mean making payment arrangements or whatever is needed to satisfy the client and complete the transaction. Keep in mind that money isn't as much about resources as it is about resourcefulness. Be creative in how you package your programs, how you make them available to your customers, and how you allow them to pay for them.

**Easy to Say Yes**

Many times, speakers present too many options and ideas, making it difficult for audience members to know what they're supposed to do as the next step. I was recently at an event where one of the speakers talked about their workshop, which sounded fun and was quite affordable. Then, the speaker started outlining all the bonuses, all the other things that you were going to get by signing up for the workshop. People lost track of what they were originally buying. It became confusing and, in the end, no one could say yes, because they didn't recognize what the next step was. Clarity in your offer is vital. Make it easy to say yes.

My staff and I endeavor to say yes to any request that our students make:

- If someone says, "Can I break it into four payments?" the answer is yes.

- "Can I give you the first payment thirty days from now?" The answer is yes.

- "Can I bring a friend and buy his today?" Well, yes.

- "Can I have you give me a call so I can give you a new credit card number tomorrow?" Yes.

Look for ways to keep people happy. Many speakers say they don't answer yes to these questions because the clients are never going to call back or make the payments. I've found the absolute opposite to be true. Saying yes has helped me build customer loyalty.

Here's the deal: if somebody's not going to give you a credit card number tomorrow anyway, maybe they didn't want to buy in the first place. I'd much rather have a class full of eager students who are ready to get to the next level than conduct a babysitting session, having to put out fires from people who regret taking the course.

You're looking to create a mutually beneficial relationship. If you make it easy to say yes, more often than not, you'll find that clients will approach you with that same spirit of: *Yes, I'd love to do this.*

The relationship is most important. You train people how to treat you. If you are accommodating, always saying yes, and always looking out for their interests, clients learn from experience that they can trust that you will always look out for their best interests.

For example, I have a couple students in my one-on-one program right now. As you remember, some people have paid about $100,000 for this one-on-one program with me.

Why have they done that?

I don't have a seminar where I sell my one-on-one coaching. I don't get up on stage and say, "I'm looking for ten people for my one-on-ones."

Instead, along the way—when clients have had a problem to solve, or they've tried to move forward to accomplish something—I've provided solutions. I've always made it easy to say yes, and I've always delivered value, so they've been happy that they said yes.

Therefore, when they ask, "What do you recommend as the next step?" I can tell them that they've gone as far as they can through these programs, and I would recommend one-on-one coaching.

Since they've always had a good, positive, *yes* experience with me, it's not a sales job anymore. They have positioned me as a trusted expert, and one who's genuinely interested in their success, always willing to accommodate their success, and always helping them be successful.

Therefore, their desire to buy is not based solely on the question: *Should I do this?*

Instead, it's based on the feeling that they know, given their history with me, that they'll be taken care of. It's no longer a debate in their minds. They know I'll help them, because I've done it so often. This is the experience you want to strive to provide your clients and potential customers.

## Predictability and Sustainability

Most speakers, coaches, and trainers have never created a budget, yet as a businessperson, this is one of the most basic needs.

What does it take to maintain or grow your business?

Most are flying by the seat of their pants. They determine the pricing first. We've discussed how to do that, in terms of establishing and assessing value, but most people engineer the process in reverse.

Their process looks like this: *Okay, the venue is going to cost me this much, there's maybe some marketing, maybe some travel, and accommodations. To make my money back and have a little bit in my pocket, this is what I'm going to charge.*

Although they are truly providing value, the tendency is either to underprice their programs or value themselves so much that they overcharge. Either way, they haven't gotten it right. You must take the time to understand your business and the business model. In our programs, we go into great detail on building the right business model for what you're trying to share.

Because most speakers have it wrong, they're not building long-term, sustainable profitability. They're always on the hunt, so to speak, for the next event to speak at and the next group of people to sell to because they've never created programs and services that are predictable and sustainable. Those two elements — predictability and sustainability — are lacking among most speakers' business plans, but they're what speakers would love most to have. Even more, I'm sure their families would appreciate that.

For any entrepreneur, achieving predictability and sustainability is tough, but now you're getting paid to share your knowledge, insights, information, concepts, and strategies. If you don't practice them in your own life by strategically planning for the growth of your business, your audience senses that, too. Your business reflects your entire life. When there's no stability there, everything will, to some degree, be affected.

What makes an event successful?

Sometimes, it can be things we haven't thought about. At some of the events I've participated in, I have had the chance to share the stage with some well-known speakers, and the money I earned was of secondary importance to me. That's been a measure of success for me. Yes, we need to make money to stay in business. That's true. But what makes an event significant to us may not be the money. In fact, money was a side note to what I experienced at those events.

## THE RIGHT AUDIENCE OVER A BIG ONE

The success of your business comes down to positioning yourself as an expert. I do a lot of teaching specifically for speakers about how to build a speaking business. Much of what I teach is hard skills and factual, results-driven material.

I teach a specific set of skills:

- How to create products
- How to increase number of speaking gigs
- How to share the stage with big names or combine for a joint venture

I've been invited, on occasion, to speak to groups that weren't my best audience. These events are often a waste of time for me and for the audience, because the tools and knowledge I'm sharing are either completely in an unrelated field or they aren't quite ready to build that for their business.

One example: I talk a lot about money when it comes to the speaking business. About a year ago, a friend was involved in a charity for raising money for kids who had suffered burns. I'm always happy to help, but my friend dictated what I should be speaking about.

She said, "All your stuff on how to grow a business, to build wealth, and all these things, that's what you need to talk about. That's what you need to bring to this group."

I followed her instructions, and I felt so bad talking about building wealth—and almost, to some degree, selfish gratification—at a fundraiser for a burn unit for children. Thankfully, I was speaking twice that night, to two audiences. So, for the second presentation, I changed my speech entirely, as it needed to be more appropriate for that audience.

One of the big traps we fall into as speakers is we believe as long as there are people who will listen, we are ready to go. That's an absolute mistake. Sure, there are many groups you can speak to. When I spoke at that charity event, I honestly think I offended people in the audience. That didn't help my brand; it didn't help them feel good about me. I didn't feel good about it in the end, either. It was an uncomfortable experience.

Having produced movies like *The Gratitude Experiment* and other films, I have a message that's more suited to them than how to make money: know your message and know your audience. Additionally, it's just as important to know who is *not* your audience. It can create big problems for you if you're willing to speak to anybody. You don't want to do that.

## Define Success

Analyze what a successful event means to you. The money you earn is only one measurement of success. Some of the best connections and relationships I have forged were at events. Once I spoke to an audience of 7,000 people in a big arena and, although I do remember what I got paid, that's not the most important thing to me. The most important thing to me that day were the pictures taken from the stage. I loved those pictures, and I would have done the event for free and covered my own airfare just to get those amazing photos of me on stage in front of that massive arena of people.

You must define what is it that makes an event successful for you. It could be something you don't usually think about. At many events, the money was secondary to me. What makes an event significant to you could be the connections you make, the clients you attract, or the opportunities that open for you.

For me, it's been pictures, connections, and relationships. Once, a young man in his early twenties came up to me with his dad.

He said, "It's really interesting that I finally get a chance to meet you. You saved my life!"

I said, "What do you mean by that?"

He said, "Well, let me tell you a little of my story."

He had been involved in drugs and had significant substance problems through his teenage years. He also had impregnated a young woman. At that time, he had troubles with the law, violence, and aggression. The girl did not want to have anything to do with him and took the baby. The parents of this young man were devastated, because they no longer had access to their grandchild. This young man became so depressed that he would steal money from his parents, do drugs, and spend most of his time sitting on the couch playing video games. The father tried everything in his power to get this kid motivated, to get out and do something with his life, and hopefully turn it around. The young man wasn't going anywhere. His dad would leave motivational tapes, CDs, and books around the house, and the kid became a bit resentful of these things.

One day, he was seriously depressed and decided to end his life.

His dad had left for work, his mother wasn't home, and he decided: *This is the day I'm going to do it. Wouldn't it be a funny joke if I took one of those CDs from these motivational people, put it in, and literally blew my head off while listening to one of these motivational guys?*

Well, as fate would have it, he picked up the one that he thought featured a man with a smug, ridiculous look on his face, with boy-band hair. Well, that was me.

He cued up the CD and said, "I'm going to blow my head off listening to this smug prick," — and I quote, this is exactly what he told me — "and everybody can see that this motivational stuff just doesn't work. It's for other people, not me."

He put the CD in and started to listen to it.

On the recording, I must have said something funny, insightful, or helpful to him, because he said, "I started laughing, and I actually scraped the barrel of the gun along the roof of my mouth, and it hurt. I literally cussed and took the gun out of my mouth, but soon after, I put it back in, and I continued listening to your silly rhetoric. After a minute, you said something, and I kind of wanted to write it down, so I put the gun down, and I went to write it down."

I thought: *If you're going to kill yourself, why would you take the time to write something down?*

He said, "You said something else, and then another thing, and then the gun in my hand became kind of heavy, so I just set it down, and I started taking occasional notes.

"Well, you said some things that were pretty fun, and you kind of got me, or understood me. I kept listening, and when that CD finished, I put in another one from somebody else, and put in another one from somebody else. By the time my dad came home, I had decided I wanted to change my life, and I knew that I could do better, be better, and have a better life than what I was settling for."

He told me he was in tears as his dad arrived home, and said to him, "Dad, I need some help. I can't do this by myself."

His father helped him check into a rehab clinic and — not instantly, but soon thereafter — he was able to address some issues and make some new decisions.

Now, fast-forward to five or six years later. The young mother of his baby had decided to give him another chance. He was so serious and determined to make changes that they stuck. They are a happy family now, married, and the young man's parents have access to their grandchild.

He then looked at what he truly enjoyed: video games. He started a game company that builds applications for smartphones.

I don't take the credit for any of that, because it's not me. I believe that God, the Universe — whatever you choose to call it — would have placed what the young man needed on his path to help him make those decisions, to bring him to where he is, but it was such a blessing to be part of that. Had my audience that day been even just him, or him and his dad, it would have been big enough for me.

This idea that we need a massively large audience to change someone's life is not true. If you're there for the right reasons — to share your message, to be transformational and inspirational, and to guide people to a better life — your audience doesn't have to be large.

By the way, this is true even when you're not sharing motivational insights or teaching people how to make personal life changes. You can find value in helping someone get answers to a business challenge they're struggling with or helping them become more productive or fulfilled. Whether it's a relationship with others or with themselves — if you're making an effective change and creating *aha* moments for people — you can find value in that, as well.

Over the years, I've done a handful of speeches at schools. It's been gratifying to receive messages on Facebook or cards in the mail, or even be recognized when I'm out and about. You can see in the other person's eyes that you've made a difference in their lives.

You can never predict the difference you'll make. A couple years ago, I spoke at a maximum-security prison in North Carolina. I didn't know anyone there. That's not a crowd I normally hang out with, so I didn't know what to expect. Two groups of people were highly affected by that. One of them was me. I had no idea what these people had been through, and I had never seen the heart of someone who's a murderer, rapist, or been involved in drugs or violent crimes. We often see these kinds of characters on TV, and we can forget that they're real people.

When I had a chance to speak to that group, I could see that some people had made mistakes that they would have done anything to take back. The lessons I learned from them—I corresponded with some of them after speaking there—were insightful to me. For example, one gentleman said that no matter what position you're in, in life you always make the best decisions available to you at the time, or that you think are the best decisions.

That was a powerful insight. Many people may not be creating success, but they're still making the best decisions they can. They're trying to do their best with what they've been given. This has made me more forgiving of the people in my own life who haven't always treated me how I thought I needed to be treated.

They were doing their best, and that makes me more forgiving.

Our visit positively affected many of the prisoners who realized they could have a more proactive life, regardless of their circumstances, and they could make new decisions based on who they wanted to be versus who they thought they were. You never know the impact that you're going to have.

At the end of the day, no one's going to ask you, "Well, as a speaker, what does your bank account look like?"

But I guarantee you're going to recognize the legacy you've created. The largest audience is simply made up of a group of individuals. When you think of it that way, and put the individuals first and foremost, it often all works out, regardless of the size of the audience.

## The Right People Are There

If you don't feel like the right people are attending your speaking events, you're not going to give your best. It's going to come across as a weak or held-back message.

There have been times when I've shared a message from the stage and I've thought: *Oh my gosh, maybe I shouldn't even bother sharing that story, because it's not going to make a difference to anybody here. Skip it, let's move on to something else.*

Most of the time, I'll share what I feel in my gut they need to hear. I may even add a story because I feel it needs to be shared with this group. I may not be sure why, but I'll share it.

And inevitably, somebody approaches me afterward and says, "I really needed to hear that."

They'll then share with me what's going on in their lives. You've got to trust that the right people will find you. The right people will resonate. The right people who need that message will be there.

If you've done your homework in terms of demographics to understand the ideal recipient for your message, the problems you solve, and the needs they have, you'll find that your call to those people will find its way into every bit of messaging and marketing you send out. Everybody you connect with will conspire to bring you the right people.

It's easy to look upon an audience and make judgments. We all make judgments, and sometimes we assume that we know how things are supposed to unfold and how they're supposed to look. But the more we try to control things, the less we achieve and attain what we seek. The more we prepare and trust, the easier it becomes. That's my philosophy: you do what you can do, leave the rest to the universe, and it will bring you the right people.

Your success in finding the right audience relies on the act of trusting. Trust that your ideal clients are there. Prepare and then leave it with the trust and confidence that you'll be okay. Audiences can sense desperation; your speech will deteriorate with desperation.

## It Only Takes One Person

Before one of my very first speaking events, I had done all kinds of marketing. I gave out free tickets at networking events, invited friends, and did anything else I could think of. The same night as my first speaking event, there was a hockey tournament playoff—I'm from Canada, where ice hockey is very popular. Our hometown team was in the final, so from all the tickets I had sent out, all the marketing ideas, from every effort I'd put forth—three people showed up. The hotel conference room I had rented was set up for fifty to one hundred people, and I had three. As you can imagine, I moved them to the front row from the various places in which they were hiding in this sea of seats. I presented absolutely the very best that I could; I presented as though it was a full house.

After the presentation, two of the three attendees shook my hand, said, "Well done, young man. Thank you," and left.

The third person stayed for a while and told me that he was the regional director or the owner of a financial services company.

He said, "One of the things I really enjoyed and appreciated was that you presented to us with exactly the same power as if the whole room had been full. The content that you shared made sense. I liked it, I really like you, and I'd like to book you to speak to our group."

I didn't think a whole lot of it, but he said, "Why don't you come to my office, and we'll talk about it?"

He ended up hiring me for a couple things. During each of the next twelve months, they hired me to speak to four or five different groups of consultants. For every engagement, I was paid $5,000. My income for the year just went up by $25,000 a month.

I had thought that the sparsely attended event was a wash, but one of the attendees increased my income by $25,000 a month. Do the math: $25,000 times 12 is not a small amount. But it didn't stop there.

The same attendee asked me if I had any books, CDs, or tapes. But I hadn't written any yet. I hadn't written a book. I told him that I had an idea for a book, and I started talking about what the content would be. It would be a quote book, and it would share 365 daily lessons that I had learned in my work, in my research with other entrepreneurs, mentors, and leaders.

He said, "I'd like to buy some of those copies and give them not only to my representatives, but also that would be useful for our clients, as well." Keep in mind I hadn't written the book yet!

He said, "Well, what would your books cost me?"

I knew already, just by doing a little bit of research, that my cost was going to be between $4 and $6 per book, but I told him, "Probably about $10 a book."

He said, "I'll take 3,500 copies."

That's $35,000 for a book I hadn't even written yet!

This one event, with only three people, earned $300,000 for me plus *another* $35,000 in book sales. A grand total of a one-hour presentation, giving it my all for three people who decided to show up on the night of a hockey final, made me $335,000.

Recently, I was presenting at an event that promised 1,700 people. It was a free ticket, so we knew there was going to be some drop-off. But when I got there, about thirty people were in the room.

I listened to a lot of the other speakers who had traveled to be at this event in Las Vegas. Some of them said, "I'm not even going to bother. You'll see me by the pool."

I heard another say, "You know what? I'm going to present, but I'm not even going to try to do an offer, because nobody will buy, there are so few people in the room."

I even heard some people say, "You know what? I'll never, ever work with that event organizer again!"

They badmouthed the organizer, made their speeches, and left.

I believe that every situation presents you with possibilities, and it's up to you to make the best you can out of every situation. I acquired quite a few regular clients from those thirty attendees. In fact, because the group was so intimate, my close ratios were very high. But the factor that was more important than the number of attendees was the event organizer. I decided to stick around and support him, didn't say anything negative, and gave it my best shot.

Since some of the other speakers had left early, he had spots to fill, so I said, "I have more content, and I'd be happy to share for you since these thirty people, they're here."

Because I went the extra mile, even for him, he's since invited me back for many of his events, and he now has the kinks worked out. His events are no longer thirty people instead of 1,700. Now, he understands how to attract people to his events, with upwards of 600 or 700 people.

Never burn your bridges. When event organizers are starting out, it's always good to support them, because when they get to the top, they'll remember who helped them along the way. My relationship with this organizer over time has been a blessing.

As a speaker, a room is often not quite what I thought it would be, whether there are fewer people in attendance or the event isn't quite as spectacular as I had envisioned or hoped. In this kind of situation, you have two choices: you're there anyway, so you can either present with all your heart, or you can bail out and be a negative person. I have found that by being positive, there are no negative situations. They *always* pay massive dividends in the future. Too many speakers are negative when things don't go their way.

Bottom line: have confidence that, even when it doesn't go perfectly, it's taking you to something better. That's been a massive lesson in my life.

A couple years ago, I was part of a speaker cruise that we were trying for the first time. We had hoped for a large number of people to attend. We had quite a few registrations; we even had some attendee's deposits, so we knew that we had around one hundred people coming.

By the time all was said and done, we had only twelve people who actually paid the full amount and got on board—and some of those twelve were the speakers. It wasn't a big group at all. There were three speakers total, myself included. One of the speakers was extremely positive, and no matter what happened, he was always excited. Honestly, he could have been hit by a car, and he would have had good things to say about it. He had a fun time, he was positive around everyone, and everybody loved him.

As far as another speaker was concerned, no matter what happened, there was nothing but negativity and complaints. Now, when I organize events and choose who will participate, I won't have that negatively geared speaker back. I'm not interested in having her on my stage. I'm not interested in recommending her to my friends. I'm not interested in going to her events. I don't believe most of what she teaches, because she's talking about how to take control of your life and make lemonade from lemons. But she can't do it herself, so I don't believe that it's possible with her.

The other positive fellow sowed a lot of seeds with people who have recommended him for other things. I have personally given him other opportunities, including some that have made him a lot of money, because I saw how he dealt with stress and challenges.

It only takes one person to create a big opportunity. Maybe *you* are that one person. If you have a bad attitude, you're going to kill a lot of big opportunities. If you carry a positive attitude, you can create a lot of big opportunities. It's not just who's in your audience that makes the difference. Often, that whole big opportunity will *be* you, because people who interact with you will remember what it was like. But you'll shut doors for yourself if you're negative.

The same thing is true with big events. Sometimes one of the big stars or keynoters thinks too much of themselves, which rubs everybody the wrong way. They will never be invited back. If the rest of the speakers who were part of the event were more accessible and down-to-earth, the participants will look for ways to interact with those people.

The one person who can turn it into a big opportunity is you. It starts with you and expands to the audience because you're the first person who's going to change anything.

Too many speakers are chasing *the big event*. They want to be seen as a big hero on a massive stage. That might be cool, but the truth of the matter is if that's why you're doing it, you're coming from a place of ego and not service. If you are not coming from service, eventually you *will* get the big stages, but in the process of seeking the big stages, and only for the reason that they're big, you're going to lose them and eventually you won't even get the small ones.

# CHAPTER TWO

---

# Speaking Fee Options

There are three options for selecting speaking engagements that will help you build your business. Traditionally, the most common is receiving a fee for speaking or appearing at an event. But there are two others, one of which may surprise you.

The three options include:

1. Being paid to speak or present

2. Speaking for free, and being accountable for your own expenses, such as travel and accommodations, and maybe some additional expenses or obligations

3. Paying to be on stage, which at first may sound counterintuitive, but there may be circumstances in which this is a great opportunity

## GETTING PAID

To stay in business, you need to get paid. While crafting and delivering a message are important parts of being a speaker, another aspect is the business of speaking. This is what gets neglected so often. The result is that even people who have valuable messages and wonderful insights to share often don't expand to their fullest earning capacity. They have not learned how to build a business that compensates them for the value they bring to others.

If you don't make a profit, you don't get the privilege of continuing in this industry. But the impact is even greater than that: as you are compensated appropriately for what you deliver, your message can be shared with larger and vaster audiences.

This is the traditional way that the speaking business has operated in the past. This model isn't used as frequently, now, except in the settings of corporate groups hiring you to speak at specific engagements. The last few for-pay speaking gigs I had were for network marketing companies hiring me for a particular event.

This model is quickly disappearing, and many speakers don't have the connections to corporate audiences. While a lot of money can be made in this category, it's not the most lucrative. This sounds counterintuitive, because most people think being a keynote speaker is the primary goal. They try to develop their materials and their marketing to attract paid speaking engagements.

While it's true that this is not where the most money is, you should not neglect this possibility. Even if you are a beginning speaker, you may find that corporations pay a fairly significant fee. I recently had the opportunity to speak at the national convention for a major franchise. I was surprised by the amount of money that they are willing to pay for speakers. So, in the right communities, it's possible that you could gain an extremely large fee.

My experience, though, has been that this is no longer the place where all the money is. Therefore, it may not be the best route to take in today's climate.

## Myths About Enough and Too Much

Most speakers struggle with questions of self-worth and how much to charge. People often charge the highest fee possible for speaking, but they haven't built the relationship with their audience enough to attract potential clients to their ongoing programs or ongoing training. Sometimes people price themselves out. The myth here is that you need to charge as much as possible for the event. That's not necessarily the best course of action. It may be more profitable in the long run to build relationships with your audience which would allow you to charge a lower fee.

Ironically, the other myth of getting paid is not charging enough, not understanding that a lot of these companies have significant budgets for their training events. I was consulting with a fast-food franchise about ten years ago. My speaking fees were quite minimal at the time, about $2,500, and that's what I planned to charge.

For some reason, when they asked me my fee, I didn't answer with my amount, I answered with a question: "What is your budget?"

It turned out that their budget for that particular meeting — with me as the only presenter — was $15,000. At that point in my career, I hadn't been paid that amount of money for one single presentation — plus, they paid for my accommodations, travel, and everything else.

This myth reflects our fear that companies and event planners won't have deep pockets to support speakers. What we offer is of adequate value and should be compensated as such. The truth is that many companies do have the funds to pay what we're worth.

## Organizers May Not Allow Selling

When you are paid directly for a speaking engagement, often the event organizer controls the operation. If they are paying up front, they may be the ones who can control your agenda. Frequently, they will not allow you to sell your products or services, or they will control what you sell. In some cases, they will sell products for you, which may include a mass discount or a revenue split on sales, which are often 50/50 but can go as high as 80/20.

When they're paying the bill, they get to dictate a lot of the terms. Just make sure you understand completely what you are and are not allowed to do.

For example, you may find they require you to:

- Hold additional mastermind groups
- Contribute to newsletter articles
- Present webinar-type conferences
- Be available for photos with attendees

Additionally, they may not allow you to:

- Collect database information from the attendees
- Use your company name and logo on any materials, including PowerPoint slides
- Hand out business cards to attendees

**Finding Paid Speaking Opportunities**

Finding potential clients to pay you for speaking opportunities is often similar to cold calling.

You're going to have to:

- Pound the pavement
- Send out marketing materials
- Rely on word of mouth

Although speaking bureaus match speakers to events, most of the time they are focused on their biggest clients, the ones that generate the most income.

Speaking bureaus have listings of different events that are looking for individuals. That's a great resource, but it is still difficult to find the people who are going to spend the money to hire you. Finding good speaking opportunities is mostly based on recommendations and personal recognition. After being in this business for ten years, and with a reasonably well-known name as a speaker, I have had only two events specifically found through a speaking bureau. Having said that, however, there are good organizations, like ProSpeakerConnect. com, that give you the power to find the people prepared to pay you.

Another aspect of paid speaking engagements mentioned earlier is that the organization may have its own agenda.

That means that when you come to speak:

- You're going to speak on the themes that *they* have

- You're going to speak to the problems that *they* want you to address
- You're going to address certain topics in a way that *they're* pleased
- You'll offer only those products and services *they* permit

You also want to agree when payment will be made. When I'm being paid for a speaking engagement, I request a deposit upfront, typically 50 percent. Typically, you'll receive the other half just before the speaking engagement. If this isn't the case, I suggest you request this arrangement. It's a lot safer. Although it's never happened to me personally, I have heard of speakers who did an event, expecting a check later in the mail, but never got paid.

It's important to have those things clearly outlined in the agreement. Many times, the event organizer will expect you to have an agreement template that they can modify with you. They typically don't have a boilerplate agreement themselves. It's imperative that you take the initiative on these business questions.

## SPEAKING FOR FREE

In this industry, everyone used to frown at the idea of speaking for free. You've taken the time and effort to develop your content, your abilities, and your platform.

So, why should you share it for free?

I have met people whose businesses have become somewhat stagnant because they're not prepared to consider this option. You don't need to accept every opportunity to speak for free—think about your *right* or *ideal* audience discussed at the beginning of this book—but there are circumstances in which that audience *is* the right group to speak to. If that's the case, speaking for free can make a lot of sense.

**Selling With a Revenue Split**

Unlike the for-pay model, the free speaking model often promotes selling your products and services. So, you *will* be invited to sell onstage, but the expectation is that it is going to be a revenue split with the event organizer.

The event organizer's responsibilities will be:

- Acquiring the venue
- Event marketing
- Staffing the event
- All logistics

However, when speaking for free at an event, we don't always consider all that we'll be responsible for, such as:

- Travel
- Accommodations
- Shipping costs for products
- Return shipping costs for unsold products

Make sure before you get involved there are systems in place to bear these costs. I have attended events before where the organizer suffered a loss, essentially going broke. None of the speakers selling products, workshops, or services there heard from them again. Whenever possible, process your own orders, with a clear agreement on how refunds will be processed and by whom. If the event organizer has hired you for multiple events, see if arrangements can be made for them to ship the products and materials to each location.

Have a clear understanding of what the event will cost before you get involved. And even though you're appearing for free, don't go into the event putting a bounty on the head of everyone, thinking you need to close *x* amount of people. Look at everyone in your audience as a potential relationship. If you don't break even on that free event, it's not always a big deal, especially if you have the right people in the room and they continue a relationship with you. Then, those events will pay off massively. Be aware of your numbers and have a plan to recoup those funds over the long term, rather than at that single event.

## Your Involvement in the Marketing

At many of these events, the organizers expect your help with marketing. They expect you to bring people in, to fill the room.

The organizer may provide you with their materials for marketing and promotion. But, it's always important to make sure that you have the freedom to alter those materials. You want to use the voice that your followers are used to hearing.

For example, a couple years ago I was speaking at an event and they invited me to promote the event, which I was delighted to do. However, their marketing materials were quite abrasive compared to my usual style of interacting with my audience. By using their marketing materials, it made some of my audience feel uneasy.

To address this, I've since added an item to my agreements saying that I'd like to have the freedom to alter or adjust any of the marketing materials so that my audience feels comfortable.

This also works when an organizer's marketing materials aren't strong and do not convert well to sales. Perhaps the advertising is even a bit misleading or unclear, so attendees are not sure what they're paying for. With the ability to alter or adjust it, as outlined in your agreement, you're able to create marketing materials that convert and also connect with your existing audience or tribe. I've even brought specifically designed postcards for promotions that we're doing.

Your goal is to fill the room:

- You're paying to travel
- You're taking time out of your schedule
- You've shipped products
- Maybe you've even created something specifically for this event

So, you've already spent some money in advance of the event, and you want to know you'll be able to cover those costs.

Certainly, there's risk in not filling the room. It's always important to know exactly the number of people who will attend. With any event I'm engaged in, I keep in regular contact with the organizer and have them update me on the numbers until the day before the event. I have, at times, canceled because the numbers weren't high enough, or I have shown up and the numbers were not correct.

When the size of the audience isn't what was promised, you might want to renegotiate on product sales. For example, if you've agreed on a 50/50 split of sales, you could possibly renegotiate to have your travel and accommodations reimbursed, before the 50/50 split. Most of the time, the event organizers feel quite badly that the event was not the success that they had hoped, and they are willing to work with you on that.

A word of warning: you may incur fees and penalties if you've agreed to bring in a minimum amount of people, and you don't deliver. I've even seen several events where, if you don't bring in a minimum amount of people, you can be excluded from the program — and that can happen even on the day of the event — or you have to pay a penalty. In other words, if you were supposed to bring fifty people in the room and you didn't, they charge you a fee to speak that day. Be sure you understand everything in your agreement with the organizer.

## Sales Minimums and Competitive Pitchfests

Event organizers — because they are trying to recuperate their funds and have a limited number of spots on stage — try to choose the best speakers, the ones who can make them the most money. Their goal is to make a profit, so often they will require you to offer products of a specific price point. Typically, the rate now is a minimum of $2,000 or more for the program or product you're selling.

Keep in mind that if there's no minimum product price, you may find hidden opportunities. As other speakers are trying to sell their $2,000 or $3,000 program, you can over-deliver by providing a valuable product or service that's a lot more affordable.

Naturally, when you've got five or eight speakers in a day, sometimes selling $2,000 programs, people can't afford to purchase all the various products and services offered. There just isn't enough room on their credit cards to say yes to everyone. Someone may resonate with you and your message, and they want to do business with you, but their credit cards are maxed out.

Affordability is one of the big challenges with these *pitchfests*. If there's not a minimum product price requirement, find something that's affordable for most of your audience.

But, if there is a minimum and the event is highly competitive, your next step is finding where on the schedule you'll be appearing. You don't want to be the first, because that's the hardest position to be in, the first person trying to get the audience to crack open their wallets. You also don't want to be too far into the program, because by then everyone has already spent their money. Negotiate a spot that works best for you.

Generally, I try to position myself on the program after someone who will not be as appealing to the audience:

- They are not a strong seller.
- Their product is not in direct competition with mine.
- Their product is very expensive, allowing me to offer something more affordable and demonstrate high value.

Paid speaking events are often the result of successful relationships with event planners, organizers, or corporate representatives. It's just as important to pursue relationships with other speakers. Being invited to free speaking events often comes down to relationships with other speakers. Many people overlook this. The speaking field is a small community. Those doing joint-venture events with free speaking opportunities are generally always great to work with.

You can run into quite a bit of ego in the speaking business, as well. We may not be as generous to others in our industry or those who speak on the same subject. We can feel like it's a comparison game, and that in order for us to be great, we need to be better than others or put down others.

Generally, those who are stinkers — who don't contribute, for example, to the marketing needed to make the event a success — get eliminated quickly.

When events don't go as planned, which might happen with the first one or two, always look at things from a positive point of view.

Once, I was scheduled to speak at a free event for a gentleman who had about 1,700 pre-registrations. When I arrived, about thirty people were actually in the room. Some of the other speakers were frustrated. They said they wouldn't speak on stage, said things about the event planner, and were very upset.

Needless to say, those who stuck around and supported him benefitted in the end. He has now figured out his groove and how to get bums in chairs. He's a successful event organizer and has maintained good relationships with those speakers who supported him through his growing pains. The other ones are no longer invited because they did not support him while he was going through growing pains.

This situation played out multiple times. When things don't turn out as planned, understand that the organizer usually hosts multiple events. If the first one doesn't succeed, they'll continue to try. Always take the opportunity to build on these relationships, rather than reacting with bad feelings and behavior.

The same is true about developing relationships with other speakers. Many speakers are not necessarily event organizers, and when they try it the first time, it doesn't always go as planned. But they get better at it. Always maintain good relationships with other speakers and organizers.

Speakers do rise in the ranks. Early in my career, I met a young woman who wasn't great as a speaker, but she had an amazing personality.

At the time, I thought: *Well, I'll keep in touch and if something happens, great.*

She is now rocking it on the stage! She has figured out her content, and she's gotten into a groove. People evolve and get better. Be careful to keep your relationships in good shape. People remember when you talk behind their back or are critical of them. We don't help people who treat us poorly.

## PAYING TO PARTICIPATE

Paying to participate in an event may sound counterintuitive. Nobody thinks about paying to participate. Many people believe that if someone is charging you to be on stage, it's either some kind of scam or not a profitable way to do business. I have found the contrary to be true.

More of these events — especially from business trade shows — are now blocking off a section of workshop spaces so speakers can promote their products and services. Professional speakers have a big advantage at these events, because some of the people participating don't have experience as professional speakers, and they don't know how what they do compares to what the speakers offer. You can come in sometimes and steal the whole show. It's crazy! Paying to speak is the newest trend, and it's where the most money is made. Yes, it's counterintuitive but this is where the most money can be made.

## Full Rooms, Less Competition

As mentioned above, other presenters at these events are not as competitive because they may not be experienced speakers. They're people who have bought a booth at the trade show, and they want to come in and speak. Even at events that are not trade-show driven, many of the presenters are typically people who are simply trying to promote a company, product, or service. When selling and sharing from the stage at a paid event, often there are not as many speakers. Certainly there are not as many A-list speakers; you'll see more at the come-for-free-and-sell events, compared with the paid-to-sell events.

If you're paying to be there, you can be sure your organizer has a marketing budget, and they're prepared to hit a home run and make the event a success. The last thing in the world that these organizers want is an empty room for a speaker who has paid them to be there. In fact, they're much more likely to have a full room. I've seen as many as 4,000 people in a room at an event I paid to speak at. It can be quite lucrative, if you know what you're doing.

## Research the Demographic First

If somebody is trying to sell you a spot to speak on stage, they're probably a salesperson first. They're going to tell you what they think you want to hear about the event, rather than what you're looking for. So, you're going to have to do the research on their demographics.

I know an individual who was hosting a big real estate expo in New York City. The truth of the matter is he represented the demographic to be something closer to what I was looking for than what it was. I paid $4,000 to speak at his event. When I got there, the audience was all real estate investors, not people who would have bought any of my programs. In a room of three hundred, there might have been two or three people who might have been a good fit for me. But the bulk of the group was not. It's very important to do your research.

Another good strategy is to speak with someone who's presented at that event previously. Ask them what the group was like, or if they have any videos or testimonials from people who have attended. It will give you an idea of some of the regulars at those events. If there's a way to see some of the booth exhibitors, if it's a trade show, you'll get an idea of the businesses that are there. Understand who your audience is and recognize the events they attend. Do your research.

## Income Opportunities

Generally, if you're paying to participate, any sales you make are completely yours. I've never encountered a revenue split in this scenario. In fact, most often, you even process your own orders, so you might want to bring a staff member to help or hire somebody from a temp agency. I love taking care of my own sales, because one of the challenges that I had doing one of the other freebie events is that someone else processed the orders, and they took all the order forms with them. It was weeks before we got that information, so we could not make immediate contact with those new clients. You can do a data capture right there in the audience for the whole group. Again, at most of these events where you're paying to be there, the organizers are forgiving and you can almost do anything that you'd like to do.

When I'm speaking at an event and have a 50/50 revenue split with the organizer, sometimes I'll hold back some of my best products. I don't want to come out with my most expensive programs, because I know I'm going to have to split half of that revenue. So, I often offer a product or service that will allow me to build relationships. Once that's established, I can bring out my best programs, which may be pricier.

When I am not constrained by a revenue split, and everything is controlled by me, I've got no reason to hold back. I'll often present what I feel would benefit the audience the most. In some cases, I've paid to speak on an expensive stage and immediately brought out my $55,000 program. And, it's converted highly because it was a focused audience. Naturally, if I'm paying and the audience is paying, the quality of the event increases.

The biggest thing is to recognize that the industry is shifting. Pay-to-participate events are more popular. Don't make the mistake of waiting for the ideal opportunities to come; create them. Too many speakers wait for their phone to ring. Don't do that! Get out there and call others, even if you've got to pay to be on stage. You'll find, if you do it right, it will return exponentially to you.

We'll talk later on about creating your own events. But in some ways, paying to participate is probably the most effective way to grow your business.

It isn't that expensive, once you run the numbers, particularly compared to hosting your own events, which requires:

- Cost of a venue
- Cost of marketing
- Cost of staffing

If I can pay for a spot at an event — even for $3,000 or $4,000 — and they're guaranteeing 500 people in the room — *Wow!* I'll take that deal every day, because it's so much work as a speaker to assemble all that yourself. It's much easier to be a speaker than it is to be an event organizer. Those are two different skill sets, which is important to recognize. It's almost like hiring an event organizer to keep you busy.

# CHAPTER THREE

_____

# Speaking at Existing Events

As a speaker, you need an audience. If you're doing it at home in front of the mirror, you're definitely doing it right, but it's definitely not going to be profitable.

The best place to start is to find events that currently exist in the marketplace, rather than creating your own. By finding existing events, you'll find:

- They have an audience that's ready to hear you
- They've got a marketing machine running
- You don't have to do any of the heavy lifting or organizing, so it's just easy

It's like driving a train. If you have to lay down the track, it's a lot more difficult than to simply put your train on tracks already there.

## FINDING EVENTS

Events are available everywhere. You can't actually go far right now without finding event possibilities. If events are already existing and running, they are great opportunities for you. And they can save you a lot of money and time, so that you're not becoming an event organizer. You're a speaker.

## Make the Most of Your Friendships With Other Speakers

You've probably heard the saying that your network equals your net worth. But there's another aspect to this: dividing the word *network* into *net* and *work*. Think of *net* as a safety net, as well. You're able to use your network of speaker friends to solve problems you run up against. They can also be a great source of finding existing events, maybe even ones they've spoken at.

If you are on the radar of other speakers, and you've built relationships with them, they will open doors for you. If your friend is speaking at a specific event, they can introduce you to those event organizers. It's an opportunity to leverage your relationship with speaker friends into creating new relationships with event planners and organizers, and even other speakers.

Remember that the other part of network is *work*. Maintaining relationships isn't something we should take for granted. If your friends are going to share events and help you, it's only common courtesy for you, on occasion, to make sure that they're getting fed by events and opportunities you know about. The more that you share, the more others are willing to share with you. In relationships, those who don't contribute are eventually eliminated. No one likes to be tied to a taker. Make sure you are the one who contributes and shares. The extent to which you share is the extent to which you're going to see a return in value.

## Social Media

Tapping into all the different social media has been useful in my career. On more than one occasion, someone has shared an event that they're speaking at on my social media timeline. If it's an event that fits with my demographic, I've often used that as the introduction to the event organizer.

I've contacted them and said, "I see that you've got this event going on. Is there any way that I could speak or be of service to you?"

Most of the time, it has turned into a possibility. But 100 percent of the time, it's turned into a favorable connection. Although I sometimes send email, I typically make a connection by phone or in person.

I asked a friend of mine who owns an advertising agency, "Where do you find advertisers for your magazine?"

He said, "Well, I go through the other magazines, and I see who's currently paying for advertising. If they're buying advertising in one magazine, it makes sense that they're possibly going to pay for ads in my magazine."

He says his conversion rate is very high.

The same approach is possible on social media. When you see a post or tweet about an event, you can approach the organizer and ask to be considered as a speaker at a future event.

Some feel that it may be overstepping your boundaries or being too bold to promote yourself to the organizer of an existing event. They're in the event business; they'll be glad to speak with you. Even if they aren't going to hire you, at least they're a good contact for you to get to know. Don't be afraid to be bold.

## Online Event Calendars and Newsletters

Using online event calendars and newsletters is similar to the social media approach. These are publicly posted events and you can approach the organizers directly. You can also subscribe to newsletters for your specific demographic. This allows you to keep up with what others are doing and what's happening in that industry.

Another avenue for marketing is to offer writing articles for newsletters. This has worked well for me. It makes it possible for you to tap into their audience, and when events are held, you're able to present yourself as a natural choice for a speaker. Those newsletters are solid gold.

Community events are a great source for identifying specific geographical locations you'd like to grow in, and they keep you tuned into your community. For example, I work a lot in London. I love London. It's a beautiful city, and the people are amazing. I'd like to do more work there. As I look for potential events, it's much easier and effective to use online community calendars — they tell you what's going on in exactly the location you're looking to develop — rather than using social media. Social media is more random and less organized. But with community events calendars, you can focus on a specific location.

Another strategy I use with community events is to group multiple events over a short time, such as during a week or weekend. If one event organizer is interested, I contact others holding events around the same time and place and mention to them that I will be in the area. I've often been booked for speaking engagements this way because they know I'm already in the area, so they're not paying for additional travel or accommodations.

Speakers who are busy stay that way because they are actively looking for events. It's one thing to sit at home, develop content, and call yourself a speaker. But a speaker is one who is always speaking. The way you stay busy is by getting invited to events. The way you get invited is to always be on the lookout for events for which you can be considered. Sometimes, you need to take proactive steps and invite yourself.

Most speakers—even the most successful ones—are *out of sight, out of mind.* That's just the way life works. It's within your power to get on stage. It's within your power to be considered for these opportunities.

Never forget: if things aren't happening for you, and your phone isn't ringing, pick up your phone and make the move—be the one to call.

## APPROACHING EVENT ORGANIZERS

It's important to know how to approach the event organizers in the right way.

They may not have experience in getting speakers:

- This might be a new opportunity for them.
- They may be newly assigned as an event organizer.
- This might be the first event that they've dealt with.

One of the big mistakes speakers make is to not approach event organizers with the organizer's needs in mind.

See if you can understand, from their point of view:

- What they're looking for
- Who they're hiring
- Why they're hiring
- The problem they're looking to solve
- Their goals

Once you have a good understanding of the position they're in, you can solve their problems with your services.

Recently, I had an experience that put me in the role of event organizer. A client in London needed a female speaker on the topic of empowerment. The speaking fee was £15,000, or nearly $30,000 at that time. They were serious; they wanted a great speaker and they were ready to go. I posted their request to my network, as well as on Facebook.

In no time, I had sixty-four comments from people saying, "Pick me! Pick me!"

In this case, I was the event organizer, the guy they needed to convince of their fit with this speaker request. People had their friends and family write in, voting for them. I was inundated. One person had close to one hundred people rallying for them to win the assignment.

Another person actually tried to bribe me, saying, "Listen, if I get it, I'm going to give you x-amount of the speaker fee."

That kind of thing never works.

My client hired me to do a job. If I had taken a bribe or something of that nature to fill the spot with someone who wasn't qualified, it wouldn't have mattered if they gave me half of the £15,000. My credibility would have been shot, and I'd never have been able to work for that organization again. That type of behavior doesn't happen as often as you think in legitimate circles.

All these people approached me from an ego base. They came from an egotistical point of view, telling me why they were a better speaker than anyone else. Some people even criticized other speakers who had responded.

Not one of them approached it correctly.

First, they should ask about the needs of the event organizer:

- What is the theme of the event?

- What is the organizer sharing, or what problems are they trying to solve for their audience members?
- What are their goals as a meeting planner?

The key is to start by trying to understand the needs and goals of the event planner. It's that simple.

## Understand the Problems They're Trying to Solve

The first step is to find out what the organizer needs; the second step is to find out about the theme and goal of the event.

Going the extra mile and doing some research before you even approach the event organizer can give you a massive advantage. I always Google an event or talk to a speaker who's been there before to understand more about the event. Then, when I approach the organizer, I'm knowledgeable and understand what they are trying to accomplish. Being prepared has made a big difference for a lot of my students, as well.

In fact, one of my students took an idea I gave him and was super successful with it. An event planner he was working with said that he was receiving many books, CDs, DVDs, and lots of other materials from speakers. In fact, so many that most of it ended up looking the same.

So, our idea was to send this event planner one ticket to a hockey game with a little note that said, "I'd like to get to know you and your company and see if there's a good fit. I want to find out the problems you're trying to solve, and, who knows? Maybe I've got some solutions. Would you join me at this NHL hockey game?"

Well, the event planner jumped at that opportunity, and they sat together, eating hot dogs, drinking beer, and cheering on the Calgary Flames. The next thing you know, my student landed an ongoing monthly contract with this company as a strategic planning coach and speaker for all their financial planners.

When approaching event planners, it's imperative to understand their problems. Being creative in your approach is a big part of it, too.

**Leverage Your Past Experiences and Products**

The biggest challenge in leveraging your experiences is not doing it from a place of ego, but from a place of humility.

These are examples of valuable things you want to leverage:

- If you've been on television
- If you have a best-selling book
- If you've been in a hit movie

Event planners understand this. But remember, it's not a matter of who can brag the most about what they've done. If you understand the problem they're trying to solve and can attach your products and services to it, it can make all the difference in your success.

For example, I just spoke at a massive real estate conference. I gained that opportunity because of my regular appearances on CNN, Fox Business, Fox, and ABC. Those company names alone sound impressive, but what especially impressed the event organizer—as she later told me—is that I sent her clips specifically related to the problems that her group was trying to solve.

In other words, yes, it's nice to be on TV. It's nice to have the best-selling book, but what do these things really mean, and what do they mean to *your* audience?

When sharing testimonials with event organizers, carefully select the ones you send. They should be relevant to that industry, individual, or event planner and—if possible—address the specific problems that group is dealing with. It's not necessary to provide three pages of testimonials or a video clip of testimonials. Sometimes it's just too much. Try to be more specific, rather than focusing on the volume of material to share. Choose the one or two that best solve the problem your client is dealing with.

Nobody likes being handed a Sears catalog of all the things you can do, have done, or products and services that you sell. They simply don't need it. Many speakers have lots of great products, but event planners get hundreds of submissions for big events.

When I was acting as an event planner for my London client, one Facebook post alone yielded sixty-four responses. I didn't have the time to read a massive listing of what everybody had done, sold, or created. Your submission needs to be concise. When you send too much material, you risk the event organizer just skipping over yours and going on to the next guy.

Make it as easy as possible for event planners. As you approach event planners, it's also crucially important that you are prepared—your website is up, your materials are ready. If you're not ready when you approach the event organizer, do not make excuses about why.

## Going the Extra Mile

Going the extra mile positions you as a professional before the event. Additionally, it often will get you invited back. Many of my repeat clients call me back again and again, simply because of their experiences with me. This is true with my students, as well. This should be the common denominator among all your activities: over-deliver. If someone is paying me, they get at least a minimum of three times the value that they're being billed for. This has been a great rule of thumb in building my success.

How can you go the extra mile?

I've often shown up at events with free products that they didn't expect, like an audio CD or book for every attendee or a free ticket to another event. For fun, I've even brought some of my friends from *The Secret* with me to an event without announcing they were going to be there and allow them some of my stage time to speak. I'll tell you, that organizer was *so* delighted, it was amazing!

Now, when the organizer is planning another event, who do you think is at the top of their list?

In terms of speaker etiquette, I've seen a bazillion mistakes that people have made along the way.

Some of the more common ones that frustrate event organizers are:

- Speakers arriving at the last minute
- Speakers interrupting the event to get their presentations set up or have their PowerPoint tested
- Speakers dictating where they should be on the schedule

Speaker etiquette dictates that you're there to serve. Since it's their event, stay in the background unless requested to do otherwise. I've seen speakers take over the event, adjusting the room temperature and asking for water to be brought to the room.

You should *not* be trying to attract attention to yourself in any way. The event organizer will do that for you, if it's required. Even though you're a speaker, it's technically someone else's event. Respect that.

Sometimes a speaker can overstep their boundaries, especially when participating in workshops or Q and A sessions happening with other speakers. I've seen speakers make themselves appear foolish when they're trying to overtake an event. It shows desperation. They're not comfortable waiting their turn and sharing their expertise when they're asked for it. Be a class act in all you do.

Event planners and meeting organizers are real people with real problems.

Their goal is to make sure that their audience:

- Has an amazing time
- Feels they got value
- Learns the things they want and need to learn

Any ways that you can help them achieve these goals are often gratefully accepted.

I was asked to speak at an event in the UK with about 12,000 attendees. In the process of talking to them about the event and how I could support them, I volunteered to do some marketing, share our database, and work with them to secure other speakers with whom I have connections. We offered to support them in any way possible. In fact, I even found them one event sponsor.

It's important to recognize that if you can be of service to these people, you'll always be someone they'll consider inviting back. You'll always be somebody they like to work with. It's a lot easier.

What's the old adage?

*It's a lot easier to keep an existing customer than to find a new customer.*

The same is true in the speaking business. If you work well with an event planner, it could bring you literally thousands and thousands of dollars every year.


## CREATING A WIN/WIN DEAL

With any kind of relationship — not just business — it's important to create a win/win synergy. Two parties who receive value out of an opportunity are more inclined to give their greatest efforts to it and also to continue in that relationship. As a speaker, it's always advantageous to develop a win/win relationship so that you've got a partner who will help you grow your business. This is potentially what an event planner becomes as the two of you work together on an event. You're both technically working on your business, and it's important that you think about it that way.

## Clarify Expectations Prior to the Event

All human frustration, challenges, and negative emotions come down to unmet expectations. People get angry when they expect something to happen, and it doesn't go that way. Their expectations are unmet and it falls apart.

It's important to clarify expectations of everything in writing, whether it's an email, a MOU (memo of understanding), or contract.

Make sure you have outlined all the details:

- Who is going to be covering certain expenses like travel and accommodations?

- Is there a speaker fee?

- Who's covering the shipping costs of transporting your products to the event?

- What are your responsibilities for marketing and promotion?

- Are you expected to be available for webinars, teleseminars, or similar activities ahead of time?

- Is your current bio and photo accurate? Check what they're using.

- How will you and the event organizer communicate prior to the event to discuss the needs of the audience?

- Is selling permitted and what, if any, are the revenue splits?

- What days are you expected to be at the event?

- Are team members invited?

- What support can you expect at the event?

There are a lot of questions that you should ask ahead of time. It's like building a house. If you know exactly the materials you're going to need and the costs, you can definitely be prepared when it comes to pounding in the first nail. If you don't, there's going to be a lot of surprises along the way, which creates unmet expectations. Take some time and develop a questionnaire. Outline the specific questions and issues you need clarified during the pre-event phase.

## Clarify Expectations During the Event

Even though an event has been planned well, sometimes things happen:

- The speaker preceding you is sick, and you're being bumped to a new time.

- The event planner overbooked speakers.

- Speakers are scheduled back-to-back with no time in between to conduct sales or have opportunities for pictures, and so forth.

At the event, clarify a number of things up front. Some of the things that I've found to be most valuable are:

- You need to have at least fifteen minutes after your speech to be able to process orders, meet with people who just heard your speech, and take pictures.

- I never do a Q and A because I need the time to transition into sales. I don't want to have a Q and A with some negative nasty in the audience that pulls the thunder out from under my sales pitch.

- Go through your bio with the organizer to make sure that it's read effectively. Your bio is not just a throwaway; it is part of your pitch. Everything — before you even get on the stage —

contributes to your credibility and how people will respond to you.

- If you have video or AV, you need time to check the equipment and make sure that it's operating effectively.

- I bring new batteries for any microphone that I use. I don't care if they were just put in that morning. Things don't always work as they're supposed to, so be prepared.

- You want to get the daily schedule, so you can understand the flow of the event. As we discussed, there are certain speakers you may not want to follow, as well as certain speakers you may want to follow. There are certain times of day that are going to work better for you in conversion than other times of day. If you can analyze and explore these types of details ahead of time, you'll be on your best game and there will be no surprises.

- Ask if there's a secondary room adjacent to where the event is happening, where you can relax and not be accosted by the attendees.

- Come as organized as possible. You may find that if an event is unorganized, you aren't able to give your best performance, either.

Most event planners—if they understand your needs in advance—are super accommodating. I've rarely had any challenges.

## Clarify Expectations After the Event

Post-event responsibilities and activities should be determined ahead of time. Some of the most useful items:

- Who will do follow up with potential clients, if needed? Sometimes having this follow-up coming from the organizer rather than you is a great way to increase your credibility and sales.

- Who's going to handle refunds or credit cards that don't bill effectively?

- Who's keeping track of sales and any revenue split?

- How can you follow up with all attendees? This is important to sell to those who weren't ready to buy at the event.

- Always debrief with the event organizer after an event to make sure they're happy. They'll know that you're concerned that they had a good and powerful event. That debrief sets you apart from other speakers and bodes well for being considered in the future for their other events. Going the extra mile doesn't go unnoticed.

One final thought: don't be afraid to suggest resources and tools you have that could make the event even better. For example, I recently spoke at an event in Florida, and I mentioned to the organizers that I had some media contacts that might be valuable for them. We brought the media there, and they took a little bit of B-roll and interviewed some of the speakers, myself included. Sometimes those little ideas make an event a little bit more exciting.

Another time, I introduced a friend of mine—who hosted a live game show— to an event planner. The game show featured people with foam mallets smacking each other in the head, and other silly things.

So, when an event planner said to me, "We'd like this to be a super fun event. Do you have any other ideas that we could talk about, do, or share?" this was a good fit.

It made the event more fun and notable. And since I was already appearing as a speaker, they had me co-host the game show, which was lots of fun. You never know what will happen, but when you make it fun for the event organizers, you make their job easy. They're bound to be interested in having you back in the future, as well.

# CHAPTER FOUR

-------------------

# Hosting Considerations

When building your own events, some speakers expect it be like the *Field of Dreams: If you build it, [they] will come.*

It doesn't operate that way in constructing events. Often, speakers simply put up one EventBrite page or an event page on a community calendar, and then are surprised when they show up and there are no lines of people ready to come in for a free event—or any kind of event.

Like anything in life, the chances that your event will turn out spectacularly, and you will be pleased with the results, are based on:

- How strategic you can be about reaching your audience
- How much you plan
- How much you work to carefully eliminate any risks—the things that could go wrong and the things that may be lacking

Most speakers assume that the content starts to flow from the minute you're on stage, and about forty-five minutes into the speech is when you roll into your pitch, and the last ten or fifteen minutes is when you focus on your pitch. The absolute truth of the matter is that your pitch begins the minute a person decides to attend your event. Everything from the initial marketing to what happens once they arrive — when they take their seats and have a chance to interact with you, others, or your staff — helps determine whether they will choose to continue a relationship with you or purchase your products. Don't take this section lightly if you choose to host your own event.

## HOSTING YOUR OWN EVENT

If you aren't speaking on stage, then you need to get yourself busy. This is one of the most popular reasons for hosting your own event. Professional speakers *speak.* Sitting at home thinking about speaking is not going to build your bank account or your business. You need to get out there and build events if you're not at someone else's event.

Although building profitability is important, sometimes building an event is more a matter of exposure. You want people to know your name and experience your presentation. This leads you into the category of speaking at other events. You need a place to begin. It's kind of a catch-22: people can't hire you until they hear you, and the way to make it happen is to let them hear you.

Most of my friends who are involved in the music business have invested in recording a demo and performing small shows, which has led to being heard by people who can sign them to a record label or give them an opportunity to perform at other venues. You must do the same. It's not enough to be speaking to yourself in front of a mirror, at home in your closet, or in a private room. You need to get on a platform where people can hear you, and one of the best ways to do that is to host your own event.

## The Risks

There are quite a few risks you take when hosting your own event. The good news is if you plan correctly and follow some of the earlier steps—identifying your audience and the problems they're trying to solve, where they're located, and so forth—you can eliminate many of them.

The largest risk is financial. You can rent a venue, put money into marketing, and spend a lot on staffing the event, even creating products and materials specifically for that event. But if you haven't marketed effectively, you'll find yourself with no one in attendance, or the wrong people in attendance, which is just as bad.

Sometimes speakers feel like they'll just do an event *on the cheap*, as inexpensively as possible, just to fill the room. Let's say you get lucky and one hundred people show up.

But when they get there, they say, "Wow, this is a crummy venue. This is not organized. I don't want to be here."

The other risk is that if you start people off with a bad experience, they won't come back. The reason people will support you as a speaker — even more than your content — is because they have had a good experience with you. Your primary connection with your audience is an emotional one. They're wowed by what you do, and they have a good experience.

Early in my career, I was organizing an event in New York City with a friend. I was excited. It was one of my early international speaking events. The event planners created a successful marketing strategy, and fifty people had registered and paid. The venue was three blocks off Park Place, famous for its affluence. However, the room they put us in did not make the best impression: the carpet was stained, as was the ceiling. Some of the folding chairs were broken. A faucet in the corner dripped.

I made an executive decision. I walked down the street while my guests were arriving at this less-than-ideal location, and I went to the Sheraton on Park Place.

I asked them point blank, "Have you got a board room, meeting room, or any kind of room, so we can move these people over here?"

Right there on the spot, I made a commitment to my audience, gave the Sheraton my credit card, got the room sorted out, and quickly met their staff. They were empathetic to our emergency, so they got on it right away.

I went back to the first seminar room, welcomed all the guests, and turned it into a lesson on first impressions. I asked them to share their experiences about how they felt when they arrived.

Then I said, "Okay, follow me, because we're now going to show you how those lessons can be implemented."

The whole group of fifty followed me a block down the street into a conference room at the Sheraton on Park Place, which was a beautiful location.

I improvised that solution out of necessity. I wanted people to have a positive experience their first time with me. Everything you do creates your brand. Taking responsibility for hosting your own event will impact your brand — people will get to know you and form opinions about who you are and what you do. Making yourself known is even riskier than taking on financial responsibility for the event. You can always make money again, but brand and reputation are hard to rescue once destroyed.

## The Benefits

One of the things I love about hosting an event is there are absolutely no limits. You can be as creative as you want to be and do anything you want to do. When it's my own event, I make sure that my audience experiences high value, but also a unique experience.

In a recent event for our Personal Power Mastery Program, because it was my own event, I was able to set up two different sets of chairs. At the back of the room was a circle for sharing activities, and at the front of the room was a classroom setting. It allowed me to adapt, move people into different settings, and share creative experiences that were highly memorable. If someone else had been coordinating the event, I may not have had the freedom to do that.

Another benefit is because you're in charge of everything financially, you also receive the financial compensations and benefits. Even when other speakers present at my events and they've sold from the stage, there's money coming back to me on their sales.

At the beginning of my speaker career, I knew that I wasn't always the strongest seller. I'm still not. I'm not one of these hard-sell guys; I'm relationship-based. I've often offset my expenses by inviting people who are better sellers than I, and they've been able to pay for my entire event and carry it.

When you create your own events, you're the one who controls the program and the flow. I'm able to position myself however I want to in the event, and that's a big benefit people may overlook.

## Logistics and Presentation

Creating a successful event boils down to preparation and execution. Many of my associates hire an event organizer or an event manager, someone who can manage all the minute details. You can focus on what you're there for, and they can focus on supporting you. Event managers are easier to find than you may think. You can hire one on an event-by-event basis, so they don't have to become a full-time part of your staff.

Over the years, I've developed a checklist for successful events. The next time you attend an event, look around the room and make a note of even the little details they've done, what is successful, or what is lacking. Start creating a checklist that you can take with you from event to event, noting what works and what doesn't.

When planning, an element that is commonly forgotten is planning breaks throughout the day. You need to plan for breaks in the program to use the restrooms or for lunch, of course, but also remember to plan breaks between your speakers. This allows them an opportunity to prepare for their time on the stage, as well as to take advantage of sales opportunities after their speech.

Everything needs to be planned; it's not just a matter of renting a room and saying: *Let's go!*

Ultimately, there's nothing more fulfilling than hosting a great event. You will feel a sense of accomplishment. It's more than just showing up at a location for a speaking engagement, selling some products, and getting on an airplane home. That's fun and exciting, but to know that you've just hosted a successful event — one that you've chaired from beginning to end — is a truly satisfying feeling. Especially if you don't have any other opportunities available to you as a speaker, hosting an event is a good strategy for success.

## FILLING YOUR OWN ROOM

Filling the room is the number one problem of speakers hosting their own event. It's the biggest challenge. Most people struggle with it. Concern about whether they can fill the room is the main reason people decide *not* to host their own events. It can be daunting.

## Why Do People Come to Events?

If we said that people attend events for information, that would be incorrect. People can find information online—videos, articles, audios, even online courses. There's much more to it than that. The word that I like to use is *connection*. People come to be part of a community and connect with those thought leaders they admire and want to learn from.

As I've attended events over the years, I've noticed many different reasons people come. But they all focus on connection. For example, a woman traveled with her son from Japan to Vancouver simply to meet me, shake my hand, and attend my event. Don't underestimate the power in this connection. Others have told me the reason they were attending an event was simply to network and meet others with similar mindsets and aspirations.

Understanding your connection to your audience—and using it as an element of marketing—can be quite powerful. We'll discuss that more in the next chapter.

People attend events because they have a problem to solve. They genuinely have a need or want. It may be a topic that, until now, they haven't been able to crack open for themselves. Often that comes down to a belief or a mindset. They want to get to a higher level than they've yet experienced.

## How Do You Present an Irresistible Offer?

It doesn't take more than a cursory look at a community calendar or Google events in your area to see that there are hundreds. I'm speaking at an event in Toronto soon and seven or eight other events are all happening on the same weekend. Maybe three or four of them — including the one I'm at — have very similar topics, and great, worthwhile speakers.

So how do people decide which event they'll attend?

You make them an irresistible offer, the one they realize will serve their needs.

The first aspect of an irresistible offer needs to demonstrate how the information they'll receive at those events is going to impact their lives and get them the results they're looking for. In addition, you can offer bonuses for people who attend the event. We often think of bonuses as things that we gift people when they make a purchase or act in some way. But the action that we're asking them to take now is simply to show up.

Valuable bonuses need to be directly correlated to your audience's interests. They want results-driven bonuses linked to the event they're attending.

Bonuses can be books, audios, or DVDs. Some speakers offer contests or raffles for special items, like iPads, but your audience won't be coming for the chance to win an iPad. Make your bonuses relevant and valuable to your audience, something they can't get anywhere else.

Irresistible offers are always structured to deliver far more value than a person is asked to contribute. Give them a reason to attend; earn the right to invite them to come. Show them why this event is going to be a stronger benefit for them than spending their Saturday at home on the couch.

Motivating people to come can be difficult. But if you get the momentum in the direction of the event, it's easier. People are often more successful with momentum than they are with motivation. Give potential attendees some tools they can learn about or an activity they can do prior to the event. We try to engage people with the content prior to an event, which has been successful for conversion. Speakers hold teleseminars and webinars to get people interested in the same way. When your potential clients are engaged—when they get value, but feel like there's far more—your chances of them coming to your event are even higher.

**Why Free Doesn't Work Anymore**

A free ticket used to entice people. They weren't paying for anything, but they were getting information and value. Two things have happened with free tickets.

First, many people register for the event, but because there is no sacrifice on their part—no investment of time, effort, or money—they feel no loyalty to it.

People who attend success seminars may feel like success is lacking in their lives. So, no-shows may not be about the information presented, or the topic of the event, but because they don't follow through on the things they say they're going to do. That's the crowd you're targeting. Unless they have made a commitment—purchasing a ticket—chances are, they're not going to show.

The stats confirm this to be true, as well. If you have 100 registrations for an event, you are *lucky* if 30 people show up! Other speakers say it's actually closer to 10 percent, so for every 100 people you want in the room, you need to have 1,000 preregistered for a free event.

The second reason free events don't work is free events attract a certain level, or tier, of thinking: *I am on the hunt for free information.*

When you try to engage them in a relationship with you and take the next steps—and there's money involved—these people already have mindset that free information is the best way to go.

I no longer speak at free events. I focus on fairly minimum-priced events and low-priced events. But

I've found that my conversions are much higher, even with small rooms. This has been true for others in the business, as well.

Even if you're selling tickets for $25, you must create an irresistible offer, giving $100 or $200 value for that $25 ticket. The fact that a person is willing to pay $25 shows they understand that they need to put some skin in the game. They need to compensate you for what they are going to receive. Their mindset coming in the room is already different than those focused on free information. They understand that sometimes it takes an investment on their part—even if it's a minimal investment—to get access to the results and tools that you'll be presenting.

Free doesn't work anymore. There are just too many free events available; there's too much noise. People also get in a mindset that a free event also equates to lesser-quality information. Therefore, the serious speakers are at paid events.

I have spoken on stage at a free event, with 300 to 500 people in a room. You can still convert at those events, but you've got to push for it. At a free event, I can close about 30 percent of the room, with a fairly accessible product priced at $197. At an event with paid tickets — even $25—my close ratios generally go up to 80 or 90 percent.

You don't want to fill the room with *fluff*—people who aren't going to serve your business. It's much more important to have the right audience, rather than a big one.

When I first started in this business, a speaker told me that if we couldn't get enough bums in chairs, we'd just paper the room. I didn't know what that meant, *paper the room*. I learned that it meant going to every event, every location, every coffee shop, and giving away free tickets. That might have worked in the 1980s and 90s, and I have been part of those paper campaigns early in my career. I don't even bother with it anymore.

The cost of printing tickets, gas to drive around town to visit all these places, and giving away tickets just didn't work. It didn't convert. And even worse: it upset the people who had paid for tickets.

You'll start getting nasty phone calls saying: *How do I get a refund on my ticket? or What's the difference between the free ticket and my ticket?*

Be careful about giving away free tickets to a paid event.

If you want to give away a couple free tickets, use a contest. Then there's a *reason* the free ticket has been given away. Be wise about how you share free tickets.

## GETTING HELP TO FILL THE ROOM

It's a big fallacy that if it's your event, you've got to fill the room by yourself. Any high level of success—whether in speaking, sports, or entertainment — is always accomplished by a team. If you're going to have a successful event, you're going to find that the greatest success comes when you get support. If you're trying to do it by yourself, it's going to be needlessly difficult. Build a team and get support.

### Affiliates and Joint Ventures

Affiliates are different than joint ventures in some ways. This is not the definition for all cases but for this section. Affiliates are partners who promote the event. They're not necessarily speakers. They could be, but they're not sharing the stage that day. These people may be potential audience members or even some of your students and clients. With affiliates, you'll want to create a program to track them and how they'll be compensated. Compensation is not always financial: it could be access to special classes, bonuses, and products. Later on, we'll talk about compensation and incentives for people helping you.

Joint ventures (JVs) are a little different. In this definition, JVs are the speakers. For example, I'm doing two events with Marie Diamond from *The Secret.* We want to sell as many tickets as we can and have as many people in the room as we can. In addition to Marie and myself, we've added four other speakers. Those four speakers are also going to help fill seats. Now, we've got a total of six people promoting the event.

We are encouraging people to provide:

- Online links so everyone can share the events
- Special bonuses and discounts for their community and their tribe to follow them
- Their own marketing materials and efforts

With JVs, I usually require participating speakers to bring in a minimum number of people, and they make that commitment. If they don't arrive at that minimum number of people, they can pay a penalty or possibly be removed from the opportunity. Most of the time, I'm careful to select speakers for my events who either have a proven track record of filling rooms, or they're someone I've worked with and know they're making their best efforts.

## Working With the Media

Media is powerful and overlooked tool speakers have in their arsenal. Think of a media appearance as if it's a pitch from the stage. The reporter will be asking the questions and so forth, but you need to demonstrate the value and results your attendees will get and then give them the ability to act.

Being on the air is a great opportunity to hold contests, because stations love to engage their listeners and give stuff away. Most TV and radio stations jump at the opportunity to give things away. Particularly if there's competition for events in your city, the moment that you get on television, it's almost as if the media is endorsing your event as the one to attend. These appearances are vital.

Another strategy to use is public service announcements, or PSAs. A number of community calendars online or on the radio make regular announcements highlighting local events.

What is the magic secret?

How do you get covered by PSAs?

It's simple. You get a charity involved — it can be as simple as a food bank, a local boys' and girls' club, the junior chamber of commerce, or a children's hospital. Set aside funds in your budget to be donated to the organizations you support. When you include a charity in your press release, it quickly becomes a valid and worthy cause to be picked up as a PSA.

Some speakers complain about donating to a charity. Many of these charities are worthy, and you always get more than you give. Recognize it as a marketing expense because that charity is going to give you thousands of dollars of exposure in your community by including you on these public service announcements.

The exposure you get from PSAs will:

- Build your brand
- Build your credibility
- Get the word out
- Help fill the seats

And you're doing a good deed at the same time.

This type of donation is not an expense at all, but an investment. One of the big keys to growing a speaking business, especially if you're a transformational leader, is to practice what you preach. You've got to give back. You've got to let go of some of the things you're holding onto tightly to be able to receive more. One of the best ways to do that is to simply start giving back to the community.

Once you've chosen a charity to support, they typically start promoting you, too. They've got databases of people and organizations they work with. They have newsletters and they will support you in getting the word out, especially if you are a regular contributor to their cause.

We support the Alberta Children's Hospital Foundation in Canada and send checks regularly to them. In fact, in my one-on-one speaker program, we have a check presentation to them every Christmas. We all put on Santa Claus hats and go to their office. It's a lot of fun. Aside from the good feelings it gives us, and the fact that we're doing good in our community, that organization makes sure that we know about any event that aligns with our mission. It's a great opportunity to secure media attention and do good at the same time.

## Using Online Support

Today, successful events use online tools to grow their businesses. The more people hear about you, the better the opportunities. Although traditional advertising like newspapers, radio, and television still work to some extent, nothing comes close to online.

Online opportunities for promotion include:

- Event calendars
- Newsletters
- Blogs
- Social media
- Pay-per-click advertising

Explore various event calendars, even ones that charge you to list an event, because those particular ones actually attract the people who are interested in that topic. Paid event listings are often higher quality than the free listings. Don't neglect the free ones, but look at the paid ones, as well.

Newsletters and blogs are highly valuable. You can find blogs that are already dialed into your specific demographic so you're not reinventing or re-establishing an audience. Some blogs and newsletters sell ad space, and if you develop a relationship with the publisher, they may promote your event on their lists and databases.

Social media and pay-per-click ads are by far the most effective because they're so easily measurable. You know how many clicks you received and what keywords drew those clicks. Then, you can adjust and build on what's working. Naturally, as you do, you start building a formula that works. It's a quick and easy way to determine what is sticking and what's converting.

I'm not computer technology savvy. I *don't* take care of many of the computer details for my business or social media. I hire an organization that has these skills, then I explain what I'm trying to do in terms of filling the event. These organizations take care of these details, monitor them, and manage them, so I'm free to focus on other aspects of the event. They can help you be successful with pay-per-click or other online marketing avenues.

If you can delegate some of the tasks involved in hosting your own event, you can focus on the most important details. If you try to do everything on your own, other aspects of your event will suffer. Don't be shy about asking for help. I'm always surprised how helpful others are willing to be. Many of them already have connections in place to make sure an event is successful; some have connections with the media. They have ideas on how to get the word out through a variety of avenues.

It's useful to get everybody who will be involved in the event on a conference call and mastermind the question: *How do we fill the room?*

You'll find some amazing things can happen.

# CHAPTER FIVE

---

# Marketing Your Events

We've talked about whom to market to and where to do that marketing. We discussed how to get help marketing. The message of your marketing comes next. Recognize, first of all, what the objective is.

What are you trying to accomplish with your marketing?

What is the next step you want people to take?

Some speakers market just for the sake of marketing, without plan or strategy: *Let's put something out there and see if it sticks.*

Marketing is a strategy, and it begins with the end in mind. Identify your end goal—for people to attend an event, buy a product, hire you to speak—and keep that clearly in mind. Then, as you invest in marketing, it will actually provide a return. I use the word *invest* specifically, because there is a difference between investing and spending. Your objective is not to spend money for the sake of spending money; it's to get a return on your investment.

## TARGETING THE RIGHT PEOPLE

You must market to the right people. There are many audiences you can potentially speak to. There are a lot of bums that can go in chairs, but the right people — the ones who can make the decisions — are the only ones who really matter in the end. Finding the right people will save you headaches and so much effort later.

To identify the right people, consider:

- Who they are
- Where they are
- How they think
- The decisions they make

If you can determine these, you will find that your marketing will be much more effective overall.

### Using an Egoic Title That Highlights the Problem

Many speakers, in their marketing, take what we call a *shotgun* approach. They use a message that blankets as many people as possible.

They use general questions, such as:

- *Are you having trouble with time management?*
- *Are you looking to make more money?*
- *Do you want to grow your business?*

These aren't powerful enough and won't even register with most people. Be very conversational in your marketing, so it *feels* like you're speaking right to your audience.

You wouldn't walk into a room and yell, "Hey everybody, who wants to make more money in their business?"

You wouldn't do that, because what would the result be?

Everyone would look at you and shrug their shoulders. As a group, people don't respond to that. But if you were to have a conversation with someone and you called them by name—if you walked into a room and said, "Hey, Scott!"—all the guys named Scott would turn and look at you directly, and they'd pay close attention. The closest you can get to calling people by name, without actually knowing or using their names, is to find an egoic title for your event.

If you had a message for all the single moms, or stay-at-home moms, or maybe all the dentists or chiropractors in the room, people could immediately identify: *Wait, that's me!*

They identify, so they respond.

Rather than a general question asking: *Who'd like to make more money in their business?* ask more specific questions:

For example, ask: *Female entrepreneurs: would you like to make more money in your business?* or *Single moms, female entrepreneurs: would you like to make more money in your business?*

The more specific you can be, the more you'll find that your audience will relate to your message, as though it's written specifically for them.

The second aspect of marketing is identifying the problems you're solving. Once you've created the egoic title you'll be using, determine the specific problems that these people are struggling with.

If you ask who would like to make more money in their business, it's too general. There are a bazillion different businesses out there with a bazillion different problems, and they all want to make more money. However, the problems faced by single-mom entrepreneurs — very specific — differ from someone who is the CEO of a real estate company. By being specific, you can pinpoint the problems those particular people find relevant to their situation. Take some time to specify your audience and make sure you include those identifications in your marketing.

**Establishing Your Credibility**

There are a few reasons people would do business with you. The most immediate one is emotional: they like and trust you. They feel that you are valuable to them, and you have their best interests at stake.

How do you create that?

Understand their problems, demonstrate that you understand, and offer solutions. As part of the solution, share how you have either dealt with a similar problem in the past, or encountered that problem in the past and come up with a solution. Experience and expertise are important to communicate in the marketing, as well.

I've seen speakers market through videos.

The effective videos generally start by asking questions like these:

- *Are you struggling in a dead-end job?*
- *Are you ready to quit your job?*
- *Do you want to have more free time at home with your kids and family?*
- *Do you want more time to do the things that you love to do?*

There are a couple of possibilities for titles there, although I wouldn't call them egoic.

But there are several identifiers to which people can respond: *Yes, that's me!*

Then those videos move on to something like: *You know what? I came from the same background. I worked in a job in the corporate world, I did this, this, and this. I found that while I was making okay money, I found that I was not satisfied in my life.*

Then they introduce a system or formula that will also help you.

Next, they encourage you to act.

By demonstrating the *Then, Now, and How* — where you were *then*, where you are *now*, and *how* you moved forward — can often establish a strong pattern of credibility. I encourage you, in your marketing, to follow the *Then, Now, and How* strategy to build credibility in your marketing.

Some speakers go overboard. They'll list how many times they've been a *New York Times* best seller, all the TV appearances they've done, the fact that they've made x-amount of dollars, shared the stage with so-and-so, or done all these amazing things. Be careful when you do that. Sometimes if you are bigger than big in the eyes of people, they don't feel it's authentic. They don't feel it's honest.

Overselling yourself is risky:

- Your audience can't relate to you.
- You're in a different world than them.
- Your solutions don't fit with their immediate problems.
- You don't understand them.

Credibility isn't about proving that you're better than everyone else, which is an egoic place to be. The whole idea of credibility is, rather, to prove that you're just like your audience, and you've got a solution to their problem.

## Building In a Call to Action

The call to action—the invitation that you're asking them to act on—needs to make it easy for people to say yes.

For example, for you as my reader, if I were to ask you right now, "Can I borrow your car?" most people—because they haven't met me in person or don't know me—will say no.

You're not going to send me your car keys in the mail. It's too big an ask. However, if we became friends, perhaps over time you'd develop trust and confidence in me because there were things you asked me for and I gave to you freely. Or, maybe you got a chance to know my family really well, and you knew that we always did things with integrity, and we always returned things we borrowed in better shape than we found them. Maybe in the past I had even loaned you my car if you needed it.

Then when I ask, "Can I borrow your car?" you're not going to have difficulty saying yes, because the experience and the trust is there.

You need to build that trust before you ask too big a thing from your audience. We always ask appropriate to what we've earned the right to ask.

In your initial marketing, you might want to consider easy calls to action:

- *Come and attend this event.*
- *Buy a low-cost ticket; come and learn more.*
- *Click here to watch a video on some tools that might help you.*
- *Click here for an e-book.*

But if, in your very first marketing touch with them, you ask them: *Come to my event! It's $4,995,* your conversions are going to be difficult to attain because the relationship isn't there.

You haven't yet earned the right to ask. Start with the easy asks and engage people in the relationship. Then you can earn the right to elevate and make the larger ask in the future.

Have faith that if your marketing is done correctly, the right people will respond. What you want, more than anything, is people who resonate with you and your message, whom you can actually serve and solve problems for. Most speakers get a little nervous when they hear this idea that they've got to narrow down and be specific with their audience. They want to speak to everybody.

When you're looking for an audience of everyone, generally you find no one. Seek specifically those who resonate. And if you've got multiple audiences, use the 80/20 rule. Focus your efforts on the ones who are your most profitable, the ones you can help the most. You can always add other demographics later.

## INCENTIVES FOR HELPERS

We all have things going on, we all have things to do, and — as one of my friends put it — we're all the stars of our own movies. We're so engaged in surviving in our own lives, we don't wake up in the morning wondering how we can put our own activities on hold and help others.

If you're going to ask others to help you, you've got to determine what's in it for them:

- What do they get out of the experience?

- What support will they get?
- What compensation will they get?

Once people recognize that you have their interests at heart, that you value their input, help, and suggestions, they're inclined to give more of it. Rewarding your helpers often equals more support.

## Why People Want to Help

One of the main reasons people want to help is that they recognize a cause that they believe in and support. They also recognize that you're an individual who they like and want to spend more time with. Money can be a motivating factor, but it's not the only one. Align with people you resonate with; those are the ones you want to recruit to help.

Most people are willing to help if you ask. Most people have a kind and giving nature, and they want to see the things that they believe in and love succeed. They *will* give that help, but here's the challenge: keeping yourself in their orbits.

When people ask us for help or referrals, why doesn't it happen?

There are three main reasons:

1. We haven't been instructed how to help. We don't think about it as we're talking to our family

and friends, because we haven't been instructed on how we *can* help.

2. We haven't been motivated to help. We haven't been given proper compensation to make it valuable enough for us to let it take up space in our minds.

3. Follow-up isn't built in. We feel like the person who asked us for help has left it alone. Without a follow-up or check-in, we have little motivation to begin or continue our efforts.

If we help others with their projects, they'll be willing to help us. People are willing to give their time and effort to help the causes that they like.

## What's in It for Them?

You want to make sure the value you're asking of the people helping you is returned to them. People get involved for many different reasons. Sometimes they might say they don't want anything in return, but everybody performs better when they're rewarded, when they receive value, support, and help.

I've done several hundred TV and radio show appearances over the years. People often ask me how I get invited to do so many. It depends on incentives. Every time I am on a television show, the very next day

I send a gift basket to the producer and the host who interviewed me.

So, naturally, if I'm a fit when they have a particular subject come up, who will they think of?

It keeps me in their minds regularly. Even when people aren't expecting a gift, recognition, or compensation, they'll be more inclined to help you if you give these to them.

As others see the gifts and the rewards you share with those who help you, they're more inclined to get on the bandwagon, too. One of the strategies we use to fill a room is to offer $20 to our key students for every friend they bring to our event. In other words, if they bring ten friends, I give them $200.

Because we presented that cash in front of the entire audience, soon our audience sizes grew even more; people wanted the recognition and compensation. As I reflect on it now, that was a great way to fill a room. This strategy has turned out to be complete marketing genius.

Think about it: if your friend brings you to an event, you already trust your friend, so when it comes time for the offer, you're more inclined to take it. Your friend also helps close that sale. Then, naturally, we offer a bonus for that friend if you decide to buy a course or program. It works well, and everybody is compensated. It has grown my business, but it also blesses them and gives them the finances and value of recognition as a contributor in helping us grow our brand.

## Organization and Tracking Compensation

Not only do you need to keep your affiliates organized, you also need to be organized with JV partners, such as other speakers. Unfortunately, I've been in situations where the event organizer was extremely unorganized and at the end of the day, he couldn't give me the orders from people who signed up specifically for my program. He had the order forms, but he hadn't written on them which courses were purchased and from which speakers. We actually had to look through the credit card bills and make our best guess based on the prices they were charged. When the event is not well organized, it's frustrating for everyone.

In compensating your assistants, if you're not organized and know which students brought which friends, it can get ugly. One assistant approached me at the end of the event and was livid that another woman was compensated for bringing in someone she felt *she* had brought. It created a challenging energy. Confusion like that can be avoided when you organize and build systems for tracking how people are coming in. There are great automated software tools available to help you do this. You don't have to reinvent the wheel. Find a program that works for you.

Make sure you compensate your team quickly after the event. You don't want to wait until months later. If they're rewarded immediately, they're more inclined to keep working for you.

The people who attend events are invited to help at many of the programs they attend. There are many opportunities for them to support the speakers they love. You may need to do some research and develop competitive incentives to make sure you are taking care of your people. If you've got better incentives than others, people will talk about you as one of the speakers who treat them the best.

## INCENTIVES FOR ATTENDEES

These principles also apply when inviting people to attend events, both your own and others.

- Why will people choose to attend your event?
- Why will they choose your speech?
- Why will they choose your event over another?

It takes more than incentivizing people to buy a ticket.

When you're presenting in a trade show setting where there are multiple breakouts, you may need a new strategy.

Remember, you need to have a solution for specific problems to compete for attendees to come to your event over other offerings.

Below are three things that have helped me attract attendees when there are multiple breakout sessions.

1.  They need to feel your event is exciting: *This is an event that I need to be at! This is going to be fun!*

    *Fun* should be a strong component of your marketing campaign. For example, a friend recently posted a video of his mastermind retreat from the previous year: a big pool party with waterslides, wave runners, music, and entertainment. The video listed some of the top speakers who were there. The video alone made me want to attend. Create excitement around your event.

2.  Big names and personalities are exciting. If you can find a reason they should be at your event versus someone else's, a great strategy is to advertise who else will be attending. Many of my speaker friends use a celebrity as a hook to grab people's attention. In fact, a friend is holding an event this weekend, with appearances by Stedman Graham, Oprah's long-time boyfriend, and John Gray, author of *Men Are from Mars, Women Are from Venus*. People want to be there

because they want to see and hear these people; these are people they admire and are excited about. Even a local celebrity is a good draw. These people are much more accessible than you would imagine.

3. *This event can really make a difference for me.* People understand that this event has the missing piece they're looking for. Your marketing needs to reflect this in a very credible way. Promote your events as highly educational, highly valuable, and delivering on their expectations.

## What Makes Your Event Unique?

You're limited only by your creativity.

Consider searching for a unique approach to the basics:

- Locations
- Times to start
- Guests
- Angles to a problem
- Requests of attendees, such as dressing as a unique character

That's what sets these events apart. They create a brand, but also create a memorable experience for your people and certainly promote word-of-mouth advertising. Take some time to see what's unique about your events.

Don't blend in with everybody else. You want people to start identifying you in a unique way.

How can you do that with your event?

You can either make your event *different* or *dynamically different.*

What I mean by different is *weird.* You don't want to create a weird event, because that could hurt your brand and work against you.

Dynamic, however, speaks of forward energy. If your ideas for being unique and different are in harmony with your brand, and also are fun, exciting, and highly memorable, go for it!

Recently, a speaker was talking about this principle of being dynamically different. He came out wearing an interesting, brightly colored, custom-made suit. Nobody had seen anything like it. In all of his PowerPoint presentations and marketing, he kept these fun elements going: a guy wearing a bright yellow suit. It supported his brand of being visible, unique, and different.

Another example of this is Seth Godin. In his photographs, he always seems to have a unique look. He's not always smiling at the camera; he's often looking off to the side. That's a great example of someone who understands the power of unique marketing, branding, and positioning. Find a way to do these little things that will define your brand. They don't have to be big, shocking things. Sometimes little things can be fun.

As another example, a speaker I interviewed for a movie impressed me with her unique presentations. Although she didn't make the final cut, I'll never forget her. Her glasses were shaped as dollar signs, and she had a magic wand with a dollar sign; these memorable strategies dovetailed with her message. The magic wand was a reminder that certain things you touch — including your problems — can generate cash. It also represented the possibility of touching it with a magical idea, magical feeling, and looking at opportunities. With the dollar-sign glasses, she taught others to have the vision of possibilities; that there was opportunity in everything. It may seem hokey, but I'll never forget it. It was a powerful lesson. Some unique and out-of-the-box ideas can really work.

## Pre-Event Activities to Increase Attendance

One thing that has increased attendance for me over the years — as I've talked to attendees at my events — is that they felt like we had a relationship before they arrived. They liked me, trusted me, knew me, and appreciated my information. You can begin to build a relationship with your audience in many ways:

- Webinars
- YouTube videos
- Daily blogs
- Media appearances
- Radio programs

Start a campaign that includes these means of interacting with your audience. Even if you don't have an event in the immediate future, start building a relationship with your audience today.

The movies we've created have *exponentially* changed my business. Those films have had a dramatic effect, opening doors and positioning me for success. People who have seen the movies make sure they're at my events. I've also written three books: *The Opus, The Gratitude Experiment,* and *The Treasure Map.* We're working on a handful of other films and we're always looking for great speakers to work with us.

Activities like these give people a chance to sample your content but, most importantly, create the opportunity to connect with you and build that connection before your events. That's the easiest kind of ticket to sell; it's not a cold lead. It's not a first contact or a first touch. It becomes almost like you're reaching out to a friend you'd like to connect with. It's so much easier.

In regard to incentives, for either your audience or helpers, remember that people don't like to be bought.

The incentive needs to feel genuine, and it needs to be authentically valuable. Look at it from their point of view. It's not just about giving something away to get something. It's not a transactional exchange, so to speak. You are rewarding people who are already excited about what you do and rewarding them in a way that's a genuine thank-you versus buying their support.

# *Conclusion*

Wow, wasn't that fun?

I know you're going to have your own experiences. You'll also have your own challenges you'll need to overcome. As those challenges come, take them on with confidence and persevere to the end.

When I asked one of my mentors about the key to his success, he said, "Some people think that success comes from doing something that's hard, but that is not true."

To him, success started with finding something he loved, and then doing it, even when it was hard.

It's the same thing with your speaking business. You have brilliance within you. You have decided that you are going to be a teacher of this brilliance to other people who need your help and your support. They have problems to solve, difficulties that you can help with, and, in some cases, you are the unique solution they are looking for.

Your perspective is unique. There are people only you can help. But there will be a day when it will be difficult. There will be times when it's not easy, and you'll feel like it's time to quit or give up. At those moments, dial back into your reason for doing this, your brilliance, and keep going—even when it's challenging. In life, there are ups and downs, but for those who keep going, ultimately, it gets easier and easier.

Life is like a J-curve. Imagine the letter J. We all start at the little hook at the bottom and when we try to start something brand new, initially we struggle, so we go down to the bottom of that J. It seems difficult. But if we persevere and keep pushing through, suddenly we get to the stem of the letter J; it goes dramatically up, quickly.

The same thing happens with everything you've learned, whether it's learning to walk or ride a bike. At the beginning you failed, and eventually you got to the point where you could ride a bike and maybe even do a variety of tricks. So, keep going! The same will be true in your speaking business. It will get bigger, bolder, and more successful, and you will be able to accomplish all the things you desire.

With that in mind, I wish you the best, and I look forward to seeing you on a stage soon!

# *Next Steps*

If you are ready to take the next steps to building and growing your speaking career, please visit my website, DouglasVermeeren.com, for free tools and strategies that you can use right away. In addition, our calendar shares all our events, where we can meet in person so you can tell me about your speaking business. You never know — perhaps one day we can share the stage together!

# About the Author

Are you ready to level up your speaking business?

Douglas Vermeeren is the Speaking Business Multiplier and the CEO of 10X Your Speaking Business, and host of the popular *10X Your Speaking Business Show.*

His tools help speakers:

- Create highly profitable speaking businesses
- Position themselves as experts
- Attract media attention
- Get publishing deals
- Get more speaking gigs
- Speak internationally
- Joint venture with other top names in the business

Douglas Vermeeren has done all this and more, and now his systems and secrets can be yours. His clients include beginning speakers all the way to movie and music celebrities, professional and Olympic athletes, top business leaders, and other speakers just like *you!*

He has been consistently rated by the media as the top speaker-trainer in the world today, with the most comprehensive and powerful tools available. Other trainers stop at presentation skills, while Vermeeren is the only one who helps you build the speaking business systems you need for success. This book is your opportunity to find out why all the top speakers are working with him!

For more information, go to DouglasVermeeren.com.